JULIE K. GILLIES

Prayers
To CALM
Your Anxious
HEART

HARVEST HOUSE PUBLISHERS
EUGENE, OREGON

Cover design by Studio Gearbox

Cover photo © KanokpolTokumhnerd / Shutterstock

Interior design by KUHN Design Group

Julie K. Gillies is represented by MacGregor and Luedeke Literary, Inc.

Prayers to Calm Your Anxious Heart
Copyright © 2020 by Julie K. Gillies
Published by Harvest House Publishers
Eugene, Oregon 97408
www.harvesthousepublishers.com

ISBN 978-0-7369-7792-0 (pbk.)
ISBN 978-0-7369-7793-7 (eBook)

Library of Congress Cataloging-in-Publication Data

Names: Gillies, Julie K., author.
Title: Prayers to calm your anxious heart : 100 reassuring devotions /
    Julie K. Gillies.
Description: Eugene, Oregon : Harvest House Publishers, 2020.
Identifiers: LCCN 2020018502 (print) | LCCN 2020018503 (ebook) | ISBN
    9780736977920 (trade paperback) | ISBN 9780736977937 (ebook)
Subjects: LCSH: Anxiety--Religious aspects--Christianity--Prayers and
    devotions. | Trust in God--Christianity--Prayers and devotions. |
    Diaries--Authorship--Religious aspects.
Classification: LCC BV4908.5 .G535 2020 (print) | LCC BV4908.5 (ebook) |
    DDC 242/.4--dc23
LC record available at https://lccn.loc.gov/2020018502
LC ebook record available at https://lccn.loc.gov/2020018503

All rights reserved. No part of this publication may be reproduced, stored in a retrieval system, or transmitted in any form or by any means—electronic, mechanical, digital, photocopy, recording, or any other—except for brief quotations in printed reviews, without the prior permission of the publisher.

Printed in the United States of America

21 22 23 24 25 26 27 28 / BP-SK / 10 9 8 7 6 5 4 3 2

For Emily and Audrey, with love.

Contents

To: Vivien Woolley
From: her friend Riley Burgett

Happy 18th
birthday!
2023

An Invitation

t's a heartbreaking reality: We're a nation plagued by anxiety, which affects more than 40 million adults in the United States.* I've wrestled with anxiety on many occasions and have family members and friends who daily struggle with anxiety's oppressive reality.

This book is an invitation to pause, to breathe, and to let your heart rest in God's calming presence. The devotions are all Scripture based, because God's Word brings the comfort, stability, and truth that will fill your heart with His peace. I'm a fan of learning by doing, so I've provided prayers you can pray to reinforce each day's verse and thoughts.

The Heart Notes section at the end of each devotion is a space for you to quiet your heart and journal your thoughts, getting your anxieties out of your head and into God's hands. It's a place to remind yourself of all that stirred your soul as you read and prayed. It's a place of praise to reflect on God's goodness, to notice even the smallest victory and remember how

---

* "Facts and Statistics," *Anxiety and Depression Association of America* (website), accessed August 29, 2019, http://adaa.org/about-adaa/press-room/facts-statistics.

God showed Himself faithful in the storm. It's an opportunity to observe your progress and God's faithfulness despite anxiety and worry. So take a moment. Breathe. And give yourself permission to rest here in Christ.

As you begin this devotional journey, know this: Though God doesn't always keep you from the fire, He's in there with you. Though you don't always escape the flood of anxiety that makes you feel like you're going under, He reminds you...

> When you go through deep waters,
>   I will be with you.
> When you go through rivers of difficulty,
>   you will not drown.
> When you walk through the fire of oppression,
>   you will not be burned up;
>   the flames will not consume you (Isaiah 43:2).

May the Lord, who is kind, meet you here. May His Spirit breathe on you as you take in these words. And may He grant you His beautiful, calming peace.

1

Unshaken

I know the LORD is always with me.
I will not be shaken, for he is right beside me.

PSALM 16:8

How would our days differ if we lived with the tangible, ongoing awareness that God's presence is literally right beside us? Would our hearts race less? Would our minds worry less? Jesus knew our lives on this earth would not be easy. That's why He said, "I have told you all this so that you may have peace in me. Here on earth you will have many trials and sorrows. But take heart, because I have overcome the world" (John 16:33).

So when unexpected family news jars our hearts, when days of multitasking overwhelm us, or when we have no idea how we're going to pay this month's rent, we don't have to despair. God *is* always with us. We are not alone. He is Immanuel, God with us (Isaiah 7:14). This means that God Himself is our ever-present stability. We can have peace in Him. Lean on Him. Count on Him. We can remain unshakable because He is our firm foundation, our Rock. And because He is always with us, we can experience the deep, moment-by-moment peace and stability our hearts crave—no matter what situations we face. We can confidently say along with the psalmist, "I will not be shaken."

Lord, sometimes my heart is overwhelmed and I struggle to find peace. Will You please increase my awareness of Your presence and help me remember that I never face anything without You? Remind me that whatever I walk through, I'm never alone. Since You are always with me and You strengthen my heart, I can entrust every concern to You. I do not have to worry. Remind me that I can lean on You and count on You; You are my peace. Help me remain aware that You are Immanuel, God with me. Thank You for enabling me to experience the beautiful peace and stability my heart craves. Because You are right beside me, Lord, I will not be shaken. In the name of Jesus, amen.

HEART NOTES

_____

_____

_____

_____

_____

2

Thought Steering

Now, dear brothers and sisters, one final thing. Fix
your thoughts on what is true, and honorable, and
right, and pure, and lovely, and admirable. Think
about things that are excellent and worthy of praise.

PHILIPPIANS 4:8

What we think about steers our lives. We can head in a good direction or a bad one, depending on where we allow our minds to dwell.

Dwelling on the negative steers our hearts toward stress and discouragement and anxiety. *I never expected this. There's no way I can deal with it. Did she really say that to me—how could she? My anxiety won't let me get out of the car; guess I'll just go back home.* Each of these thoughts takes our minds to an upsetting, distressing place. A place where anxiety increases and interferes with our peace.

But what if we prayed first, asking the Lord to help us reframe our circumstances and think differently? How might that change our feelings? *I never expected this, but God will give me wisdom and grace to deal with it. Did she really say that to me? Then she must be hurting; I will forgive her and pray for her. My anxiety wants to keep me in the car, but I'm going to make the effort anyway, with faith that God will be with me and help me.*

Dwelling on what is true, honorable, right, pure, lovely, admirable, excellent, and worthy of praise recalibrates our hearts and points us in a life-giving direction. It keeps our thoughts healthy and allows inner calmness to increase. It fills our minds and hearts with hope and light and truth and peace.

Lord, will You please help keep my thoughts from veering in bad directions that foster anxiety? Teach me not to dwell on the negative but to pray and ask for insight. Whatever I face, let me reframe it by Your Spirit so I can respond differently. Teach me to focus on a fresh, God-honoring, life-changing direction. Help me think about what is true, honorable, right, pure, lovely, admirable, excellent, and worthy of praise. Thank You for the reassurance that as I fix my thoughts here, my heart is recalibrated, my anxiety is diminished, and my mind is filled with hope, light, truth, and peace. In Jesus's name, amen.

HEART NOTES

_____

_____

_____

_____

_____

3

Venting to God

I pour out my complaints before him
and tell him all my troubles.

PSALM 142:2

Believe it or not, God wants to hear our complaints. We do not have to hide them or hold them in. He knows our hearts anyway (Romans 8:27), so attempting to conceal what is bursting inside us is not only unnecessary, but pointless. Bottling up our grievances, disappointments, and hurts is the exact opposite of what King David did (just read the Psalms!), and he was a man after God's own heart (Acts 13:22). When David struggled with fears, uncertainties, insecurities, and injustice, he poured out his heart to the Lord. Candid and honest, he expressed all that was in his heart, and we can do the same.

We can express our deepest hurts and disappointments and entrust all that is in us—the good and the bad—to the Lord. His heart toward us is kind, and He longs to be the safe place we run to when we need to vent. He loves us, understands us, and longs to be gracious to us (Isaiah 30:18). When we pour out our troubles to Him, He holds us close. He hears us, gives us insight and godly perspective, and quiets our hearts.

Lord, when I feel concerned or upset or grieved about something, may my first response be to pour out my heart to You. Help me not keep things bottled up but instead come to You and share my emotions and heart unreservedly. Thank You for being the place I can run to when I need to vent. God, You are always available, and You know my heart. When I tell You my troubles, You always hear me, You understand, and You soothe me. You give me insight and clarity and godly perspective. I'm grateful I can pour out my heart to You at any time and take comfort in Your abiding presence. In the precious name of Jesus, amen.

HEART NOTES

_____

_____

_____

_____

_____

4

Inseparable

I am convinced that nothing can ever separate
us from God's love. Neither death nor life, neither
angels nor demons, neither our fears for today
nor our worries about tomorrow—not even the
powers of hell can separate us from God's love.

ROMANS 8:38

What if we went through our days knowing that nothing can separate us from God's love? What if we forever kept at the front of our minds the fact that no matter what happens (an argument, distressing news), God still loves us with an everlasting love? No situation or person can change that. That means that no matter where we go or what we experience, God's love still covers us.

Those very real concerns making tears erupt? They cannot come between us and God. And they will never diminish His great love for us. This unfailing love is a precious gift He lavishes on us and will never be snatched from us. What a staggering, deeply reassuring truth. As the psalmist declares, "How precious is your unfailing love, O God! All humanity finds shelter in the shadow of your wings" (Psalm 36:7).

Understanding that absolutely nothing can interfere with or stop God's great love for us creates deeply secure, peaceful hearts. We can sink our toes into the warm, soft sand of God's amazing love, allowing our souls to rest there.

Lord, thank You for increasing my understanding and belief that nothing can ever interfere with or separate me from Your amazing love. No situation, no words, no misunderstandings can ever keep me away. Thank You for Your precious, unfailing love. Not even the powers of hell can separate me from it! Give me an ever-increasing awareness of how Your love fills me, surrounds me, covers me, and protects me. Help me walk consistently in the peace and confidence that Your great love provides. May I be ever convinced that nothing will diminish Your love for me. In the remarkable name of Jesus, amen.

HEART NOTES

_____

_____

_____

_____

_____

5

The Chain Snapper

He led them from the darkness and deepest gloom;
he snapped their chains.

PSALM 107:14

Anxiety can feel like a heavy chain wrapped around our minds and hearts, holding us to the very places we do not want to be. This may be our current reality, but it doesn't have to remain that way. The good news is that God is greater than any shackle. Through Christ Jesus, He frees us and lifts us out of the places of "deepest gloom." He does this by leading us, and we must choose to follow Him—not our fears. Not our angst. Not our discouragement. We can choose to remain chained, or we can choose to be led by the One who loves us.

Remaining stuck is tempting because getting unstuck requires effort on our parts. And yet, He invites us to rise. As Isaiah 60:1 (NIV) says, "Arise, shine, for your light has come, and the glory of the LORD rises upon you." We don't rise in our own strength, but in His. We rise into the reality of His affirming love. He offers us His hand and leads us "out of darkness into His marvelous light" (1 Peter 2:9 AMPC). Though darkness may claw at our hearts, Jesus, the Prince of Peace, snaps our every chain. He rescues us, covering us and flooding our hearts with His supernatural peace.

Lord, when my mind and heart feel chained, holding me where I do not want to be, lead me toward freedom. Help me not remain shackled but instead take Your hand and rise in Your light. May I always choose to follow You instead of fear or disappointment or anything else. You are my steadfast help, greater than any shackle, and nothing is impossible for You. You lead me out of darkness, out of gloom, and into Your light-filled presence. You are my hope, my shield, my fortress, the One who rescues me. You rescue my heart over and over. Thank You for never leaving me and for freeing me from every chain that produces anxiety. In the powerful name of Jesus, amen.

HEART NOTES

_____

_____

_____

_____

_____

When Life Is Harder than You Ever Imagined

I have told you all this so that you may have peace in me. Here on earth you will have many trials and sorrows. But take heart, because I have overcome the world.

JOHN 16:33

Life can be complicated, frustrating, and way harder than we ever imaged, but this should hardly surprise us. Yet it often does. Many of us are guilty of expecting an easy, stress-free life. It's tempting to yearn for a life of ease, where all our concerns unfold happily and smoothly. Yet life is not a 30-minute sitcom. And Jesus warned us not to expect problem-free lives, going so far as to point out that we would endure suffering, sorrow, and disappointments.

So when our child is suspended from school, our debit card is stolen, or we have a humdinger of a fight with our spouse, we can remain undaunted. Because it is here—in the middle of *harder-than-we-ever-imagined* times—that we can experience God's perfect peace. We can take courage because Jesus conquered the world (and all its ugliness) for us. Whether we are frustrated, frightened, or feeling the sting of harsh words, we can face reality, take heart, and even "be of good cheer" (John 16:33 KJV), knowing our Prince of Peace stands with us and overcame the world, depriving it of the power to harm us.

Lord, please forgive me for expecting and even longing for a problem-free life. Help me not expect life to be without stresses but instead face reality by Your grace. Thank You that even as I'm walking through complicated, frustrating, flat-out hard times, I can also take heart and be of good cheer. I can accept and walk in Your perfect peace because You are with me. May difficulties no longer surprise me, and may I continually take courage in knowing You overcame the world and deprived it of the power to harm me. In the powerful name of Jesus, amen.

HEART NOTES

_____

_____

_____

_____

_____

First Place

Dear children, keep away from anything that
might take God's place in your hearts.

1 JOHN 5:21

If we're not careful, anxiety can bump God right out of His rightful position at the center of our hearts. This happens when we are hyper-tuned in to our problems, focusing more on our fears, worries, and concerns than on Him. Anxiety wants us to accommodate it and give it the place of preeminence in our lives so that everything we do and plan revolves around it. But we do not have to allow that to occur. Through prayer and God's Spirit revealing the sometimes-painful facts to us, we can search our hearts and ask Him to help us remove anything that might take His place.

Letting go of all that stokes anxiety in our souls is never easy, but as we turn to the Lord and ask for grace, He helps us. We can learn to focus more on truth than on our dilemmas. We can spend more time in worship than in worry. We can learn to resist anxious thoughts, reciting our favorite Scripture verse instead. And we can bow our hearts to the Lord, humbly inviting Him to be first in our lives.

Lord, I am determined to keep You in the primary place in my heart. Will You please show me anything that competes for Your position? Whether it is worry or fear or anxiety or simply my own desire for comfort, help me stay away from anything that might take Your place in my heart. Lord, I open my heart wide to You and invite You in. Help me focus on truth and worship. Expand into the place of Your preeminence, displacing all that is not of You. Give me wisdom to resist putting anything in Your place and fill me with Your light and truth and love and peace. In the wonderful name of Jesus, amen.

HEART NOTES

_____

_____

_____

_____

_____

The Voice of Wisdom

All who listen to me will live in peace,
untroubled by fear of harm.

PROVERBS 1:33

There are lots of voices out there—voices of confusion, voices of anger, voices of division. Many voices do not speak truth, yet are heard loud and clear. And then there is the voice of wisdom. Personified as the voice of a woman in Proverbs 1, biblical wisdom leads us toward truth—toward Jesus. Wisdom calls out for us to listen, imploring us to hear and grow in understanding. It points out the right way to go and warns us to avoid spiritual and moral dangers. Wisdom helps us recognize the wrong voices and steers our hearts toward God's voice.

As we listen to and heed wisdom, we grow in discernment and understanding, which enables us to make life-giving choices. Through wisdom we learn to listen—consistently—to God's voice, becoming increasingly familiar with it so that it becomes instantly recognizable to us. Wisdom also acts as a restraint, helping us avoid strife and frustration and quarrels.

God offers us wisdom because we desperately need it. It guides and directs us, steering our hearts toward life, toward Him. When anxiety bubbles up inside us, wisdom enables us to consistently walk in peace, unafraid of harm.

*Lord, I need wisdom. Please give me ears to hear what Your
Spirit of Wisdom is saying. Help me discern Your voice
above all others, listening to and heeding wisdom. Help
me recognize when a voice is not Yours so I do not follow
it. When I hear the voice that causes anxiety or confusion,
anger or division, or anything else that is not of You, help me
turn away from that and back to You. Thank You that Your
wisdom leads me toward truth—toward Jesus—and causes
me to grow in discernment and understanding. Thank You
for helping me remember that You are always with me and
that as I listen to the voice of wisdom, I will live in peace,
unafraid of harm. In the mighty name of Jesus, amen.*

HEART NOTES

_____

_____

_____

_____

_____

Prayer over Worry

Don't worry about anything; instead, pray
about everything. Tell God what you need,
and thank him for all he has done.

PHILIPPIANS 4:6

Why do we find it so hard not to worry? We fret, get upset, and stress out. We think of everything happening in our lives that we can't control, and then we think about it some more. And our anxious hearts knot even tighter. But instead of nurturing and indulging these negative (and oh-so-human) tendencies, what if we turned every fret, every worry, and our many stresses into prayers? How free would our hearts feel? How clearly would our minds function, uninhibited by the worries that typically cloud them?

The Lord invites us to lift every worry, every fret, and all that creates stress to Him, releasing each—in their entirety—into His capable and loving hands. When we tell God all the details that concern us and all our needs, we can then focus on cultivating thankfulness. Thankfulness has the power to change the very atmosphere of our hearts. Nurturing gratitude fills our hearts with encouragement and joy and honors the Lord. It shifts our focus from what worries us to what blesses us. It displaces stress and brings to the forefront all the good in our lives, enabling us to treasure and appreciate God's kindness toward us.

Lord, please teach me to turn my frets and worries and stresses into prayers. Help me lift every stress and every worry into Your faithful and powerful hands. Teach me to cultivate a thankful heart. Lord, I treasure and humbly appreciate Your kindness. Help me shift my focus from what worries me to all the blessings You have provided. When anxious feelings arise, please prompt me to pray. By Your grace I am going to turn my worries into prayers, inviting You into every situation and releasing every concern to You so my heart can be free. As I do, thank You for holding me in Your supernatural peace. In Jesus's name, amen.

HEART NOTES

_____

_____

_____

_____

_____

A Beautiful Exchange

Then you will experience God's peace, which exceeds
anything we can understand. His peace will guard
your hearts and minds as you live in Christ Jesus.

PHILIPPIANS 4:7

t is a holy cause and effect—after we make the decision to
turn our worries into prayer (as we did in yesterday's devotion), *then* something supernatural occurs: We begin to experience God's abundant, situation-defying peace on a daily and
even moment-by-moment basis. That's because instead of
nurturing our woes, we're praying and releasing each specific
worry into God's hands. Though releasing our troubles isn't
necessarily our natural response (or easy to do), we can train
ourselves to recognize a heavy heart—which is our cue to dis-
engage our minds and surrender our worries to our good and
kind heavenly Father.

As we refuse to embrace our worries by telling God everything we need, openly and intimately sharing the deepest concerns of our hearts with Him, we are then able to focus on
cultivating grateful hearts. We do this by noticing the many
gifts He has given us. Every blessing, "every good and perfect
gift" is from our Father (James 1:17 NIV). Whether it's a full
pantry or a full plate, a working car or a ride to work, healthy

children or grandchildren or even the simple ability to take a walk through our neighborhoods—these are all gifts from Him. Releasing every worry and thanking God for all He has done and everything He has given us transforms our hearts from heavy to light, from stressful to peaceful.

What a beautiful exchange!

Lord, please help me recognize when my heart is heavy and I need to pray and release my worries into Your faithful hands. Help me be open and honest with You, sharing the deepest concerns of my heart with You and understanding my need to let go of all that weighs down my heart. Then help me take stock of all the gifts and blessing You've given me. May I notice each one, and may gratitude become second nature for me, erupting out of my heart night and day. Thank You for Your peace that passes all understanding, which guards my heart and mind in Christ Jesus. In His powerful name I pray, amen.

HEART NOTES

_____

_____

_____

_____

_____

11

Everything God Has Promised

I will not leave you until I have finished giving
you everything I have promised you.

GENESIS 28:15

There are two things of which we can be certain: God is always with us, and His promises for us will unfold exactly as He intends. How comforting and absolutely reassuring! We don't have to go it alone. And we don't have to succumb to fear; God is with us. Isaiah 41:10 says, "Don't be afraid, for I am with you. Don't be discouraged, for I am your God. I will strengthen you and help you. I will hold you up with my victorious right hand." And the Lord follows through on what He says because He is faithful. As 1 Thessalonians 5:24 says, "God will make this happen, for he who calls you is faithful." Indeed.

What a relief to know that God does not do things halfway. He does not leave us hanging. He may allow us to endure trials for a season, but He does not leave even one of the affairs of our lives permanently unfinished. "For God has said, 'I will never fail you. I will never abandon you' " (Hebrews 13:5). He is our constant. Our hope. Our source. Our joy. The Lord remains by our side, watching over our hearts and every promise He

31

has given us. In His goodness and faithfulness, He remains our steadfast companion. Most importantly, despite how circumstances sometimes appear, He ultimately will give us everything He has promised.

Lord, I'm grateful that You are constantly with me, watching over everything You have promised. You are my steadfast Rock, accomplishing Your will and Your plans and Your purposes in me and for me and through me. When my heart feels uneasy because things aren't happening as I thought they would, I do not have to worry, because You never leave Your work unfinished. You are always with me, overseeing every one of Your plans. Thank You for enabling my heart to rest in the fact that You never leave me or forsake me. Help me continue to believe that You will faithfully give me everything You have promised, including Your joy, Your grace, and Your amazing peace. Thank You for Your faithfulness, Lord. In Jesus's name, amen.

HEART NOTES

_____

_____

_____

_____

_____

12

Rescued

I trust in your unfailing love.
I will rejoice because you have rescued me.

PSALM 13:5

I f we're honest, there are seasons in which it is a real struggle to trust God. Whether it feels like our marriage is disintegrating, sudden panic attacks are randomly shaking us, or we are overwhelmed by keeping up with the house and the kids and everything in between, anxiety can make us feel powerless and hopeless. King David understood those feelings well. In Psalm 13:2, he laments, "How long must I struggle with anguish in my soul, with sorrow in my heart every day?" It's a question many of us wrestle with. And yet in verse 5 we see that David makes the decision to trust in the Lord's unfailing love. He actually rejoices because God has rescued him. And we can do the same.

Regardless of where life currently finds us, we can choose to trust God, and we can choose to rejoice. We have many things for which we should be grateful. God Himself rescued us from our former lives when we did not know Him. He rescued us from a meaningless life.

This meaningful psalm ends with David's entire perspective changing. In the final verse he says, "I will sing to the LORD because he is good to me" (verse 6). David recognized that God is always good to us, not only when our lives are easy. He truly has rescued us. And because He is good to us, we too can sing songs of gratitude to Him.

Lord, thank You for Your unfailing love. Thank You for rescuing me from my past, from a pointless life, and from an eternity separated from You. When I struggle with anguish in my soul, help me choose to trust You anyway. Thank You for calming my inner storms and helping me maintain an eternal perspective. May I always see and sense Your goodness with a grateful heart. Thank You for enabling me to experience Your peace and a calm mind and heart. You fill my life with love and hope and meaning. Help me continue to trust You and cultivate gratitude for all You have done. Help me always remember that You have already rescued me and that You will continue to rescue me from anything that would separate me from You. In the strong name of Jesus, amen.

HEART NOTES

_____

_____

_____

_____

_____

A Song in Your Heart

I will sing to the LORD
because he is good to me.

PSALM 13:6

Singing in gratitude to God throughout the day continually brings us back into His reassuring presence. This radically alters our days, taking them from ho-hum to holy. A song of thankfulness honors the Lord and lifts our spirits. It displaces our worries and bumps stress right out of our hearts. It attunes our souls to His presence, which brings us into solid and holy alignment.

When we take time to praise God at various moments (like while we drive, as we vacuum, while we walk)—recognizing His kindness, His goodness, and His many blessings in our lives—a divine shift takes place: our hearts are recalibrated and the very atmosphere of our hearts is transformed. And isn't that exactly what our anxious hearts crave? To be radically altered so they're no longer taut and stressed, but soft and pliable and relaxed and at ease?

A simple song flowing out of our grateful hearts ushers in God's presence, which dispels all darkness and fills us with supernatural encouragement, joy, and peace. Because He truly

PRAYERS TO CALM YOUR ANXIOUS HEART

has been good to us, may grateful songs constantly bubble out
of our hearts.

*Lord, will You please put a song in my heart today—and every
day? Realign my heart and fill it with praise for You. May idle
moments turn into times of worship to You, and may anxious
thoughts dissolve as I sing. May the songs of my heart radically
transform me, honor You, and encourage my soul as I focus on
Your many attributes. You are slow to anger. You are gracious
and compassionate. You are holy. You are perfect. Help me
cultivate a genuinely grateful heart. Help me constantly
sing songs of gratitude to You, Lord, because You truly have
been so good to me. In the precious name of Jesus, amen.*

HEART NOTES

_____

_____

_____

_____

_____

Asking for Blessing

May the LORD bless you
and protect you.
May the LORD smile on you
and be gracious to you.
May the LORD show you his favor
and give you his peace.

NUMBERS 6:24-26

Regardless of what is on our schedules today or how many unexpected interruptions or issues stir up anxious feelings, we can ask the Lord to bless and protect us. In fact, we must! Because God loves us with an everlasting love (Jeremiah 31:3), and because we can come boldly before His throne of grace (Hebrews 4:16), we can ask the Lord for the beautiful blessing in today's passage. It will make all the difference in our day.

God's heart toward us is kind and compassionate, and His love and faithfulness cover and protect us. He understands what we are walking through and longs to be gracious to us (Isaiah 30:18). He knows when we face difficulties and longs to be our source of strength, hope, joy, and serenity. He longs to give us His favor and peace.

Armed with these outstanding truths, let's allow our hearts to turn toward Him in expectation. However our day happens to unfold, we can rest in the beautiful truth that He is a good heavenly Father. When we ask Him, He blesses us, protects us, smiles on us, is gracious to us, and covers us with His peace. What priceless gifts!

Lord, whatever happens today, whenever anxious feelings are stirred, I choose to come boldly to You in great expectation. I ask You to bless and protect me in all that I do. As I come and go, allow me to sense Your very near presence. May my heart relax and rest in Your gracious kindness today. Thank You for smiling on me and being gracious to me. Thank You for Your kind heart toward me and for being my source of hope, joy, and stabilizing serenity. Thank You for protecting me, giving me Your favor, and filling my heart with Your peace. In the wonderful name of Jesus, amen.

HEART NOTES

_____

_____

_____

_____

_____

The Lord Fights for You

The LORD himself will fight for you. Just stay calm.

EXODUS 14:14

What a relief to know we do not have to fight our battles alone. In fact, sometimes we do not have to fight them at all. When all appeared lost as the Egyptians hunted the Israelites, God told Moses that He would handle the situation. He promised that He Himself would intervene and fight for His people. All they had to do was remain calm.

God invites us to do the very same. This means resisting the urge to defend ourselves. It means choosing not to engage in yet another conflict, fighting to get our way. It means that even in our most upsetting moments when we can scarcely breathe, we make the decision to remain calm and trust our good heavenly Father to fight our battles for us.

Sometimes our biggest battles are simply trusting the Lord and staying calm, especially when everything in us wants to stress out. Life is not always painless, and plans don't always take place as we hoped or intended. But through misunderstandings and uncertainties, God Himself fights on our behalf. What solace! God literally steps in to do what we cannot. All we have to do is take a deep breath, allow our hearts to be calm, and trust Him.

Lord, when everything in me wants to rise up and fight and totally defend myself, will You please help me stay calm and trust You instead of stressing out? I'm grateful that I do not fight my battles alone. I am thankful that even when worst-case scenarios play out in my mind, I can trust You to handle what I cannot. Please help me not overreact. When life doesn't go as planned, through misunderstandings and uncertainties, help me remain calm, knowing You are powerful and able to intervene and give grace. You are my Rock, my champion, and my defense. Today, I choose to trust You, breathe in Your peace, and remain calm. In the strong name of Jesus, amen.

HEART NOTES

_____

_____

_____

_____

_____

Fearless

Though a mighty army surrounds me,
my heart will not be afraid.
Even if I am attacked,
I will remain confident.

PSALM 27:3

We can possess a rich confidence in Christ that does not yield to fear. Our confidence cannot depend on all aspects of our lives going according to plan (because when does that ever happen?). Our confidence cannot depend on perfectly happy times. There will be days and even seasons when we are surrounded by a vast army of problems that far surpasses our ability to face.

Yet even when it feels like we're caught in the line of fire, we can remain confident in God's ability to defend us. We can call on Him, and He will help protect us. Psalm 50:15 tells us, "Call on me when you are in trouble, and I will rescue you, and you will give me glory." When we are anchored in Jesus, the One who strengthens and stabilizes us, our hearts will not bow to fear. We will ever and always bow to Him, our strength and our defender, the One in whom we can always remain confident.

Lord, help me not give in to fear, worry, or anxiety. Help me truly know You, Jesus, and develop a rich confidence in You instead of having a meltdown over my current problems. Lord, thank You for being my firm foundation. When I'm in trouble, all I have to do is call on You. You are powerful and mighty. And even when a vast army of problems hits hard, I will not be afraid. May my heart never bow to fear but ever and always bow to You, my strength. Help me walk in peace and stability because I am confident in You, Jesus. In Your name, amen.

HEART NOTES

_____

_____

_____

_____

_____

17

Out of Reach

He will conceal me there when troubles come;
he will hide me in his sanctuary.
He will place me out of reach on a high rock.

PSALM 27:5

It is a rare week when trouble of some shape or form doesn't come, unexpected and uninvited, into our lives, raising a ruckus. Loved ones go to heaven, leaving us to cope without them, hurting and shaken. Misunderstandings pierce our souls. Disappointments usher in anguish.

And yet when trouble arrives, we do not have to panic or surrender our joy and peace. When we turn to Him, God Himself conceals us, hiding us in the protection of His peaceful presence. Our hearts are safe there, in the secret place of the Most High (Psalm 91:1). He is our sanctuary, the safe place we can always run to for comfort, protection, and peace. We can hide ourselves in Him, breathing in deep gulps of His presence. Trouble may bang against our hearts, making us tremble on the inside, yet God lifts us far above it all, placing us on the solid rock of Jesus, out of reach. There, we are safe. There, we can rest. There, our hearts can be at ease.

Lord, You know the hurts and heartaches I currently face.
When troubles come, please help me not panic but instead
run straight to You. God, You are my source, the sanctuary
to where I can run for comfort and peace. Thank You
for hiding me in the protection of Your peaceful presence.
Shelter me from the ruckus disturbing my heart, and
lift me out of the enemy's reach. With You, Lord, I am
safe. I can rest. My heart is at ease, and I can breathe in
Your amazing peace. In Jesus's powerful name, amen.

HEART NOTES

_____

_____

_____

_____

_____

18

Sweet Relief

Can all your worries add a single moment to your
life? And if worry can't accomplish a little thing like
that, what's the use of worrying over bigger things?

LUKE 12:25-26

Why *do* we worry, when Jesus pointed out that worrying cannot accomplish even the smallest thing? It won't cause answers to materialize; it won't change the facts; and it certainly won't put us in a better state of mind. Worrying is actually practicing our fears, rehearsing them until they feel entirely too real, which then creates even more to worry about. It is a pointless cycle that demonstrates a lack of faith. It would help us to remember that our faithful Father cares even for something as seemingly insignificant as flowers (Luke 12:27-28), so He will certainly take care of us and each of our concerns.

How reassuring to know that God loves us and provides for us. Philippians 4:19 says, "My God will meet all your needs according to the riches of his glory in Christ Jesus" (NIV). We do not have to be troubled and unsettled, because our Father already knows all our needs—and He cares for us. Let's choose to lift our worries to Him, relinquishing each one into His faithful and capable hands. It is then that we will experience the sweet relief of His peace.

Lord, please teach me not to give in to worry. Help me train my heart to resist practicing my fears and instead trust with a simple faith that You are my provider and You care about all that concerns me. Help me cultivate a vibrant and active faith that always chooses to trust You. Help me to believe that You are involved in every aspect of my life, so I do not have to worry. Right now I relinquish every worry into Your capable hands. I know that if the flowers of the field are beautifully clothed and birds are provided for, You will surely do the same for me. In Jesus's name, amen.

HEART NOTES

_____

_____

_____

_____

_____

19

You Are Known

O Lord, you have examined my heart
and know everything about me.
You know when I sit down or stand up.
You know my thoughts even when I'm far away.

PSALM 139:1-2

What a remarkable fact: The Almighty God who spoke all of creation into existence knows everything about us. Intimately. He knows our routines down to the smallest detail. He examines the deepest part of our hearts. He knows our thoughts, exactly where we are in life, and all that we are struggling with on the inside. He knows the season we are in. He knows about our petty jealousies and the anger issue that continues to pop up despite our best efforts. He knows when we wrestle with anxious thoughts and when those thoughts affect our bodies.

God knows us well and yet He still loves us deeply. He doesn't know us and then reject us. He knows us and accepts us. He examines our hearts and then offers us forgiveness, hope, and freedom. When we feel anxious and unsettled, He knows. He understands. Being known and understood so accurately, so intimately, by the lover of our souls is an immense comfort and a beautiful gift.

Lord, You are amazing. You know everything about me and every detail of the inner workings of my heart. You understand all my thoughts—I'm never misunderstood by You. You know all my plans, my comings and goings. You know when I feel anxious or unsettled, and even then You are with me. You help me and offer me Your peace. When I struggle or sin or hurt, You give me grace and forgive me and bring healing. I'm grateful that You truly know me, more intimately than anyone else. Thank You for comforting me with these remarkable facts. May my heart be ever open to You. Help me seek to know Your heart, Lord. In Jesus's name, amen.

HEART NOTES

_____

_____

_____

_____

_____

20

Your Refuge

The LORD is good,
a strong refuge when trouble comes.
He is close to those who trust in him.

NAHUM 1:7

When our hearts are anxious and disturbed, this rock-solid fact remains: The Lord is good. Let's pause right here and allow our hearts to steep in this reassuring truth. God is good. And He remains reassuringly close to us. Close when we are upset. Close when we ache. Close when we receive unpleasant news.

The Lord is a strong refuge—not a flimsy one. Not a temporary one. He is our firm, dependable, faithful, permanent, and loving haven. He is the shelter our hearts yearn for. He is our place of safety, a divine fortress where we can always hide. Whatever issues concern us, His good plans for us remain intact. He guards us and watches over us. And He remains a beautiful, secure place of refuge for us when circumstances make our hearts quiver.

God is close to those who trust Him—that's us! Say it out loud: "Though my heart is troubled, I choose to trust You, Lord."

Lord, You are so good. You are kind. Please teach me to trust You and run to You when troubles come. I lift to You all that currently troubles my heart and entrust each situation into Your capable and loving hands. Thank You for watching over me and protecting me. You are a beautiful, strong, and secure place of refuge for my heart. You are my haven, my place of safety, and my divine fortress. As I trust You and run to You, Lord, calm my heart and emotions with Your peace. In Jesus's name, amen.

HEART NOTES

_____

_____

_____

_____

_____

21

Triumphant

"No weapon forged against you will prevail,
and you will refute every tongue that accuses you.
This is the heritage of the servants of the LORD,
and this is their vindication from me,"
declares the LORD.

ISAIAH 54:17 NIV

N o weapon." Not a single one. Ultimately, the weapons used against us—whether gossip or slander or injustice or painful wounds or accusations or any other heart-wrenching circumstance—will not succeed. This does not mean those things won't happen, but that they will not succeed in making us insecure, unstable, or fearful. In fact, we will triumph in spite of them.

This is a beautiful benefit of belonging to the Lord, sort of like having access to the armor He also supplies. Ephesians 6:11 explains that He provides us with all we need to deflect every blow of the enemy. We are to "put on all of God's armor so that you will be able to stand firm against all strategies of the devil." We have this armor because God loves us and knows we will need it. When weapons explode around us, the Lord Himself will enable us to maintain our spiritual equilibrium, joy, hope, and peace. These precious gifts belong to us because we belong to Him.

Lord, thank You that even when weapons are used against me, they will not expand and spread into my soul. I am grateful that my rightful heritage as Your precious child means that even when hostile attacks of any kind come, my hope, joy, security, and peace will remain intact because You help me live securely in You. You are my fortress, Lord. You provide all I need. You cover and protect me and bless me with wholeness and vindication. You enable me to deflect every attack and, ultimately, I will triumph because I belong to You. In Jesus's name, amen.

HEART NOTES

_____

_____

_____

_____

_____

22

Never Abandoned

Those who know your name trust in you,
for you, O Lord, do not abandon
those who search for you.

PSALM 9:10

There are times God feels far away and our desperate hearts cannot sense His reassuring presence. Honestly, I think it's something we all experience, and it's crucial to remember that when God's perceived absence leaves us feeling abandoned, we can choose to believe that, despite our current feelings, He remains near. We can choose to trust His Word instead of our emotions.

Whether we're experiencing illness or relationship disappointments or excruciating weariness of soul, He remains near us. We may not sense His presence, but He loves us with an everlasting love (Jeremiah 31:3) and never turns His back on us. He sees our desperate dependence on Him, and He knows what it costs us as we choose to continue to trust Him despite how we feel.

God is faithful, and as King David declares in our key verse, He never abandons those who search for Him. Even when our hearts grow weary and we're ready to give up because we don't have it in us to seek Him, He is faithful and remains steadfastly near. Hebrews 13:5 reminds us that "God has said, 'I will never fail you. I will never abandon you.'" What a priceless and soul-reassuring truth!

Lord, even when You feel far away and my heart cannot sense Your comforting presence, help me remember that Your love for me is constant and unswerving. Help me remember that despite what I feel, You are still near. You gave Your very life because You love me and value me. I'm grateful that You are faithful, Lord, and that You will never abandon me. Teach me to trust You and depend on You even when I cannot sense Your presence. Remind me of Your faithfulness. Help me remember that You know and understand all I'm going through. Oh God, soothe and calm my heart with the soul-assuring truth that You never leave me. In the awesome name of Jesus, amen.

HEART NOTES

_____

_____

_____

_____

_____

23

Your Every Cry

Lᴏʀᴅ, you know the hopes of the helpless.
Surely you will hear their cries and comfort them.

PSALM 10:17

S urely you will." These comforting words encircle our
hearts, reassuring us that God hears our every cry. He
knows when we're in pain, when we're anxious, and when we
feel completely helpless. However stuck or overwhelmed we
may feel, we can know this: The Lord knows how desperately
we need Him, and He understands the strain in our hearts
when our hopes are a long time coming. He comforts us as a
mother consoles her distraught child (Isaiah 66:13).

God also knows every hope in our hearts. Even the hidden
ones tucked so deeply inside that even we can scarcely articu-
late them—the very hopes that we feel helpless to achieve. He
knows how powerless we are to bring about these treasured
hopes by our own strength. But we can entrust every fragile,
tender hope incubating in our hearts to the Lord. He hears
our every cry. In His kindness He continuously comforts and
encourages us. How reassuring that He hears our cries and,
when we turn to Him, steps in and brings a precious calmness.

Lord, You know all my hopes and desires, even the ones about which I feel helpless. You know me better than I know myself, and You understand every longing of my heart. I'm grateful that You always hear me; You hear my every cry. You are near me, and Your very real presence comforts me. You understand my longing for healing, for wholeness, and for relief from the anxieties that churn in my heart, and I entrust each one to You. Thank You for establishing my way and for encouraging and comforting and calming me by Your Spirit. Lord, You are my hope. In the mighty name of Jesus, amen.

HEART NOTES

_____

_____

_____

_____

_____

24

More than a Conqueror

Amid all these things we are more than conquerors and
gain a surpassing victory through Him Who loved us.

ROMANS 8:37 AMPC

The apostle Paul endured unimaginable opposition: beatings, hunger, multiple shipwrecks, imprisonment (1 Corinthians 11:23-27). When we too endure "all these things"—a rebellious child, an uncertain diagnosis, a falling-out with a friend—we can either sink into anxiety or we can ascribe to the same mind-set Paul held.

He considered himself more than a conqueror. In fact, Paul considers all of us who endure "all these things" as more than conquerors. And we are! Not because of anything we have done, not because we've got it all figured out, and not because we are strong. We are more than conquerors because of Christ's victory on our behalf.

When we are tempted to think of ourselves as losers, or when our anxiety levels rise and we struggle in our faith, we can take a holy pause and rest in this truth: Because of Christ's great love and the finished work of the cross, we're actually winners. Jesus's victory ensured ours. And we can rest in the incredible truth that His triumph is our triumph.

Lord, as I walk amid "all these things," please help me not sink into anxiety or discouragement but instead remember that because of the finished work of the cross (and despite how I feel at any given moment), I am more than a conqueror. When my anxiety levels rise and I struggle with my faith, may Christ's mighty accomplishment resonate in my mind and buoy my heart, enabling me to stand in this truth. I will not allow myself to walk in defeat but will stand as a victor, secure and righteous and free, because of what Jesus accomplished on the cross. Thank You, Lord, that Your victory ensured mine and that Your triumph is my triumph. In Your mighty name, amen.

HEART NOTES

_____

_____

_____

_____

_____

25

Yearning for God

Seek the Lord and His strength; yearn for and seek
His face and to be in His presence continually!

1 CHRONICLES 16:11 AMPC

Our ability to walk in all the richness and freedom we desire will never come through sheer determination or mere will. If that were possible, then no diet would ever fail, fear would never win against us, and we'd all be wildly successful in every area where we long to be. But human skill and capability only get us so far. That's why Scripture implores us to seek the Lord and His strength. Once we humbly grasp how frail our abilities truly are, we start to gain understanding of how greatly we need the Lord.

We're admonished to "yearn" for Him, to desire Him above all else. Our strength is feeble. It gives out on us. Our strength evaporates when we need it most; it disappoints us. But God's strength is limitless. He is the endless reservoir from which we draw. As we seek Him with the goal of dwelling in His presence, our hearts are deeply touched. As we devote more of our time and energy toward pursuing Him, we learn that He is our rock-solid, dependable source that never fails. That His power is abundant and limitless and more than enough. That He is and will always be the strength of our souls. That in our most anxious moments, He lavishes His strength on us.

As we seek and trust Him, He brings the comfort and freedom for which our hearts long.

Lord, above all that I seek, please give me a holy yearning to seek You and Your strength. Apart from You I can do nothing, and my strength is no match for all I face—so Lord, give me a heart that follows hard after You. Give me the desire and discipline to consistently and always pursue You. You are the reservoir from which I draw. You are my rock-solid, dependable source, and Your strength is limitless. Thank You, Father, that Your presence softens and strengthens my heart, equips me for every task ahead, and brings me beautiful comfort and freedom. In the awesome name of Jesus, amen.

HEART NOTES

_____

_____

_____

_____

_____

26

Priceless Gifts

He who did not withhold or spare [even] His own Son
but gave Him up for us all, will He not also with Him
freely and graciously give us all [other] things?

ROMANS 8:32 AMPC

We witness God's amazing provision and generosity through His willingness to give up His precious only Son, Jesus, for us. Our good heavenly Father generously gives us *all* the things we need. He lavishly provides us with many priceless gifts—like joy in daunting circumstances, encouragement when our hearts wilt, and peace when we are anxious or afraid. The Father could have kept Jesus for Himself. He did not have to share His Son, but His love for us compelled Him. *That* is how much we mean to Him.

God is the giver of "every good and perfect gift" (James 1:17 NIV). He gave us Jesus, and He also graciously gives us many other gifts, such as fresh, cool breezes, warm sunshine, the beauty of a bird's song, the joy of a child's smile, a lovely cup of hot tea, and (praise the Lord!) indoor plumbing. And He gives us so much more. In our most difficult seasons, He blesses us with joy, encouragement, and peace, exactly when we need them. He provides for all that our souls need because He loves us immensely.

Lord, Your generosity amazes me. Thank You for loving me so much that You gave up Your Son for me. Thank You that You have provided everything I need through Your amazing sacrifice: eternal life, joy, encouragement, and peace. Thank You for Your kindness in providing so many other blessings in my life. I specifically thank You for_____. When my heart is anxious or afraid, help me remember that You are my good heavenly Father who withholds nothing from me and graciously gives me everything I need, exactly when I need it. In the awesome name of Jesus, amen.

HEART NOTES

_____

_____

_____

_____

_____

27

God Is at Work

We know that God causes everything to work together for the good of those who love God and are called according to his purpose for them.

ROMANS 8:28

What a reassuring truth! There is absolutely nothing we go through that God cannot work out for our good. In His sovereignty, He strategically establishes His plans and purposes concerning everything in our lives: both the good and the bad. How comforting to know that we can trust Him because the Lord is compassionate (Psalm 145:8) and cares about what concerns us; He is our defense and fortress (Psalm 62:2), the safe place where we can rest our weary and over-whelmed hearts; and He is merciful and gracious (Psalm 116:5), forgiving our many sins and lavishing His love and kindness on us.

When upsetting news hits us hard, Psalm 118:7 helps us keep an eternal perspective: "Yes, the LORD is for me; he will help me." When we feel confused, disappointed, or hurt, what an immense encouragement and relief it is to know our faithful King is with us and helps us. More than that, He is always working (John 5:17). He sees the big picture and, regardless of what occurs in our lives, He is not stymied, nor are His hands tied.

God is all-powerful, and He causes *everything* to work together for the good of those who love Him (that's us!).

> *Lord, as I walk through events that are unexpected,*
> *undesired, and confusing, please help me remember that*
> *You are kind, compassionate, merciful, and at work in*
> *everything. Thank You for orchestrating every detail to suit*
> *Your plans and purposes in me, for me, and through me.*
> *You are faithful and sovereign, and You know that I love*
> *You and have divine purpose on this earth at this specific*
> *time. I'm grateful that You've got my current situation and*
> *me in the palm of Your hand. Thank You for working out*
> *everything for my good. Help my heart rest at ease in You,*
> *my faithful and powerful King. In Jesus's name, amen.*

HEART NOTES

_____

_____

_____

_____

_____

28

Well-Armed

Put on God's whole armor [the armor of a heavy-
armed soldier which God supplies], that you may
be able successfully to stand up against [all]
the strategies and the deceits of the devil.

EPHESIANS 6:11 AMPC

My guess is that not one of us would walk around an active battlefield without some form of protection. Our sanity would be questioned and our safety severely compromised. We may not live in a country where bombs are dropping, but regular life frequently involves intense battles nonetheless. And our enemy uses effective artillery—bringing confusion to our minds, agitation in our hearts, and hindrances against our plans, to name a few of his attacks.

But God provides specific spiritual armor for us so that when we use it—understanding each piece's purpose, allowing it to be real and applicable in our lives—we can stand successfully against the enemy's strategies. The belt of truth? It helps us recognize and refute lies. The breastplate of righteousness enables us to guard our hearts; through it we know we stand blameless before God. The shoes of peace illustrate our ability to walk in supernatural peace even while dodging bullets. The shield of faith enables us to deflect doubts and the enemy's accusations. The helmet of salvation? It covers our minds and helps us think accurately and biblically. The sword of the Spirit is Scripture, living and active and sharper than any two-edged sword (see Hebrews 4:12), and with it we not only defend ourselves, but we also go on the offensive through prayer.

As we are faithful to apply God's armor to our lives, we will never get caught on a battlefield unaware.

Lord, thank You that, in Your wisdom and goodness, You have provided me with everything I need to stand successfully against all the strategies and schemes of the enemy. I do not have to surrender to his attacks; I can withstand every scheme, every evil plan, and every fiery dart. Teach me to use the belt of truth, breastplate of righteousness, shoes of peace, shield of faith, helmet of salvation, and sword of the Spirit. Thank You for this divine provision. Help me understand how vital it is for me to use every piece of armor. Help me faithfully apply these spiritual protections so I am never caught on a battle ground unaware. By Your grace I will use this armor daily, for through it my mind and heart and very life are covered. In the strong name of Jesus, amen.

HEART NOTES

_____

_____

_____

29

God's Pledge

Though the mountains should depart and the hills
be shaken or removed, yet My love and kindness
shall not depart from you, nor shall My covenant
of peace and completeness be removed, says
the Lord, Who has compassion on you.

ISAIAH 54:10 AMPC

Absolutely nothing can cause the Lord to remove His love, kindness, and peace from us. Whatever might rattle us, whatever may shake our hearts, we can take great comfort in this: God's covenant of peace and completeness—His pledge, His promise to us—can never be removed from us. Talk about heart security! When we experience physical pain, a long hoped-for desire falls through, or we struggle with loneliness, His love and kindness continue to surround us, comfort us, and uphold us. It stands as a barrier between us and despair.

This particular covenant is a holy pledge given by the Lord Himself, assuring us that when everything around us is shaking, His promise of peace isn't going anywhere. It is still 100 percent ours. Loss cannot steal it. Adversity cannot destroy it. What a treasure! What a gift! God's concern and compassion for us never cease. Even when calamity brings confusion and hurt,

His love for us will never waver. And His stabilizing peace will always belong to us.

Lord, thank You for the heart security, comfort, and inner stability that I experience because of Your steadfast promise. No matter what rattles me or shakes my heart, help me rest in the fact that absolutely nothing can remove Your love and kindness from me. Thank You for Your love and peace that cover me even as I deal with difficulties. Your love and kindness and peace are always, always mine and can never be taken away. Whatever I face, both now and in the future, these treasures belong to me. May my heart be reassured and strengthened by this truth. In Jesus's name, amen.

HEART NOTES

_____

_____

_____

_____

_____

30

Lavished with Goodness

How great is the goodness
you have stored up for those who fear you.
You lavish it on those who come to you for protection,
blessing them before the watching world.

PSALM 31:19

King David, the author of Psalm 31 (and many other psalms), had serious insight and a deep appreciation for God's divine provision. He discovered what more of us need to know: God has a vast amount of goodness stored up for those who fear Him—and that means *us*. What a remarkable truth. We can imagine immense heavenly storehouses set aside for God's people—a massive, divine abundance of goodness that God Himself generously pours out onto us as we seek Him for protection. What an extravagant demonstration of His great love.

Psalm 119:40 says, "Renew my life with your goodness." Right when we need it, precisely when our anxious hearts cry out for relief and encouragement, we can run to Him for assurance and covering, and the Lord lavishes us with His beautiful and bountiful goodness. He renews our very lives. He delights in blessing us, His precious children, with mercy and love and joy and peace—as the world around us watches and observes His goodness.

*Lord, You are so good. My heart is overwhelmed that
You have stored up a vast amount of goodness for me
because I fear You. Teach me to come to You when I need
protection from all that disturbs my heart. Thank You for
renewing my life. Thank You for lavishing me with Your
awesome goodness, mercy, kindness, and especially peace—
right when I need it. Thank You for Your extravagant
demonstration of generosity and goodness being poured
out in my life. I pray that those around me will take notice
and be led to You as You bless me. In Jesus's name, amen.*

HEART NOTES

_____

_____

_____

_____

_____

31

Don't Stop Knocking

Keep on asking, and you will receive what you ask for.
Keep on seeking, and you will find. Keep on knocking,
and the door will be opened to you. For everyone
who asks, receives. Everyone who seeks, finds. And
to everyone who knocks, the door will be opened.

MATTHEW 7:7-8

t is tempting to think that we should only pray about something once, instead of "bothering" God about it over and over. But Scripture actually tells us the opposite. We're encouraged to continue asking, to continue seeking, to continue knocking. This requires perseverance and confidence on our part. We cannot allow ourselves to give up and stop praying simply because we've not yet received an answer.

We don't have to think we're disturbing the Lord when we pray about something more than once. Because He loves us with an everlasting love (Jeremiah 31:3) and because we are His precious children (1 John 3:1), we can approach the Lord with assurance. In fact, Ephesians 3:12 says, "Because of Christ and our faith in him, we can now come boldly and confidently into God's presence." Over and over, if necessary. When we do so, we're obeying Him, pursuing Him, and desiring His intervention.

So it's okay to cry out for relief from anxiety daily, or even moment by moment. As our prayers continue, our faith will grow, our character will mature, and we will learn to depend more on God. Eventually, in His timing, we will receive His answer.

Lord, please give me great boldness to come to You in prayer as many times as it takes. Give me the holy tenacity to continue praying about all the longings and desires in my heart—the yearning for freedom and healing and wholeness, for starters—and to keep asking, trusting that You hear every word. Thank You for loving me with an everlasting love. Thank You that I can approach You with assurance and come confidently before You. You value my words, and You are always at work, even if Your timing and my timing are different. I ask that Your deep and abiding peace cover and fill me, displacing every anxious thought. Bring freedom from anxiety and all its effects. Give me grace to persist in prayer and to pursue You. In the mighty name of Jesus, amen.

HEART NOTES

_____

_____

_____

_____

_____

32

Never Impossible

With God nothing is ever impossible and no word from
God shall be without power or impossible of fulfillment.

LUKE 1:37 AMPC

t is a startling fact and not one our human minds can easily
grasp, and yet it is true: *Nothing* is impossible for God. Not
the circumstances that appear hopeless to us, not the situations
that discourage us, not the issues that repeatedly fill our hearts
with angst. When we grasp this and ask God to help us believe
it, our hearts are filled with holy hope.

Every word from the Lord and every promise He has given
us are possible because His power is greater than that of any
other. His very words contain unfathomable power. Psalm 33:9
tells us: "When he spoke, the world began! It appeared at his
command." The words God utters prosper and accomplish
exactly what He desires. Isaiah 55:11 (AMPC) says, "So shall My
word be that goes forth out of My mouth: it shall not return
to Me void [without producing any effect, useless], but it shall
accomplish that which I please and purpose, and it shall prosper in the thing for which I sent it."

Our hearts can rest in this amazing truth: Because God
oversees each word, sovereignly fulfilling each one, we can pray
bold prayers to Him—for whom nothing is ever impossible.

Lord, You see the circumstances that make me feel hopeless, the situations that discourage me, and the issues that create angst and upset in my heart. Yet not one of these things rattles You because nothing is impossible for You. Thank You for speaking words of life into my heart. Help me breathe in and believe Your Word over anything else, to believe You are able to do the very things that appear impossible. So right now I will thank You for filling my heart with a deep, abiding calm. I cannot face this, but You can. Thank You for Your power at work in my heart and life. I'm grateful that nothing is impossible for You, my faithful King. In Jesus's name, amen.

HEART NOTES

_____

_____

_____

_____

_____

33

With All Vigilance

Keep and guard your heart with all vigilance and above
all that you guard, for out of it flow the springs of life.

PROVERBS 4:23 AMPC

No one on the entire planet has the ability or authority to guard our hearts except for us. It is our responsibility, and we should take it seriously. When we guard our hearts, we act as rightful gatekeepers, deciding what we will allow to affect and influence us. For instance, we can wisely guard our hearts against worries or anxious thoughts, prevent critical words from lodging, and ward off lies before they take root in us.

We can also guard our hearts through wisdom concerning relationships, circumstances, what we read, and what we watch. We exercise discernment by carefully regarding people and situations as we're led by the Holy Spirit. It's a divine balance we walk out by God's grace, learning to trust Him wholly while using our God-given discernment. In this way we spare ourselves avoidable hurt, fear, and anxiety.

But we can completely entrust our hearts to the Lord. We never have to guard ourselves from Him, because He is 100 percent trustworthy. He is our safe place. Our hearts are always completely secure with Him, and we experience the most peace when we remain near Him.

Lord, help me walk out the divine balance of guarding my heart vigilantly and entrusting myself wholly to You, day by day. Help me use wisdom in my relationships and in what I allow into my life through screens and media and books. Give me discernment so that I do not open my heart to wrong or detrimental things, wisely guarding myself from fears, anxieties, and lies. Fill, lead, and guide me with Your Spirit so that I walk in ever-increasing wisdom. God, may my heart always be open and soft to You. You are utterly trustworthy, the safest place for my heart to be. In the precious name of Jesus, amen.

HEART NOTES

_____

_____

_____

_____

_____

34

The Lord Will Help

Commit everything you do to the LORD.
Trust him, and he will help you.

PSALM 37:5

t is easy to feel anxious and overwhelmed by circumstances, especially on crazy days when we're being hit from all directions. Sick child? Check. Flat tire? Check. Work deadline that just won't wait? Check. And yet, God's Word offers such simple hope: When we choose to trust Him, He helps us. This means that instead of struggling to manage everything in our own strength, we choose to pray, trusting God to provide and intervene in our situations and help us. It means that instead of relying on our plan, we surrender to His, which is always best. God then gives us great grace—and in His gracious kindness, He steps in.

It sounds almost too easy, but when we choose to trust the Lord, He really does help us. He helps us remain patient. Remain calm. Remain wise. Remain brave. He comforts us right when we need Him and enables us to hold it together when we're on the verge of coming unglued. He loves us and longs for us to turn to Him. Psalm 46:1 says, "God is our refuge and strength, always ready to help in times of trouble." Thank

God! He is our safe fortress, He is always with us, and He always helps us.

Lord, when my heart is overwhelmed, teach me to trust You anyway. When crazy days hit hard and I'm on the verge of coming unglued, help me remember to pray and continue to trust You. God, You are good, You are faithful, and You are my source. You are my refuge and strength and my help in troubling times. Thank You for giving me grace to remain calm and brave and for intervening in the situations that concern me. I'm grateful that You consistently show up, bringing encouragement and Your deep, abiding peace to my heart right when I need You. In Jesus's name, amen.

HEART NOTES

_____

_____

_____

_____

_____

35

Undisturbed

A calm and undisturbed mind and heart are the
life and health of the body, but envy, jealousy,
and wrath are like rottenness of the bones.

PROVERBS 14:30 AMPC

Our minds and hearts can either be an oasis of tranquility or a source of pain and drama, and both serenity and upset affect our bodies in very tangible but different ways. The key to a "calm and undisturbed mind and heart" is choosing where we permit ourselves to focus.

When we allow our thoughts to veer off course and dwell on the wrong things by comparing ourselves to others or allowing jealousy or wrath (or any other sin) to accumulate in our hearts, we open the door to sin, and that affects us physically. The consequences of these sins are like "rottenness of the bones." The New Living Translation declares that "jealousy is like cancer in the bones"—yikes! Those are some serious repercussions.

Through our focus, however, we can transform our thought life so that instead of harming us, it benefits us. We can choose to focus on "what is true, and honorable, and right, and pure, and lovely, and admirable. Think about things that are excellent and worthy of praise" (Philippians 4:8). We do this when we recognize errant thoughts and redirect them. This nurtures an undisturbed mind and heart, and our physical bodies will then reap the benefits of life and health and deep, abiding peace.

Lord, with all my heart I want to walk in the reality of peace with a calm and undisturbed mind and heart. Will you please help me avoid dwelling on thoughts that produce envy, jealousy, and anger? Help me resist the urge to compare myself to others. Help me not allow wrath or any other sin to build up inside me. Give me grace to recognize unhealthy thoughts and redirect my focus onto what is true, honorable, right, pure, lovely, admirable, excellent, and worthy of praise. Teach me to nurture wise thoughts, living an emotionally healthy life and walking consistently in Your peace. As I do this, may my body flourish with life and health. In the healing name of Jesus, amen.

HEART NOTES

_____

_____

_____

_____

_____

36

Right Beside You

The Lord stood with me and gave me strength.
2 TIMOTHY 4:17

What a deeply encouraging truth: When we are overcome with anxious thoughts, overwhelmed by grueling loads, on the brink of collapse from sheer weariness, the Lord Himself stands with us, giving us the strength to do all He has called us to do. The apostle Paul penned this verse in reference to enduring a trial while utterly alone. No advocate accompanied him. Not a single person helped or stood beside him (2 Timothy 4:16).

Few of us will be called upon to engage in a court battle without any assistance or support. But what a comfort to know that whatever we face, like Paul, we are never truly alone. From court battles to family drama to heavy burdens no one else knows we carry, our good heavenly Father sees it all, understands our distress, and calms and supports us. We are not given to despair and we are not discouraged, because God Himself stands right next to us, imparting divine strength to our hearts, minds, and physical bodies. He gives us the energy, strength, and stamina to stand and continue standing. He is our help "in times of trouble" (Psalm 46:1), and He is always with us.

Lord, when I feel overwhelmed by anxious thoughts and grueling loads, feeling so weary I'm on the brink of collapse, help me remember that I am not alone and You are right beside me, my source of help. I'm grateful that whatever I face, I am not alone. You are always with me. I do not have to conjure up my own strength, because You stand with me and offer me divine strength. Lord, strengthen me so I can walk in courage and remain solid when quakes occur around me. Instead of giving up, let me stand and keep standing, accomplishing by Your great grace all You have for me to do. I am not given to despair, I am not discouraged, and I am not alone, because You are steadfast, right beside me. Thank You, Lord. In the strong name of Jesus, amen.

HEART NOTES

_____

_____

_____

_____

_____

37

Bequeathed

Peace I leave with you; My [own] peace I now give and
bequeath to you. Not as the world gives do I give to you.
Do not let your hearts be troubled, neither let them
be afraid. [Stop allowing yourselves to be agitated
and disturbed; and do not permit yourselves to be
fearful and intimidated and cowardly and unsettled.]

JOHN 14:27 AMPC

When Jesus departed from earth, He bequeathed His peace to us. Prior to His crucifixion, when He knew He was leaving this world, Jesus announced this priceless bequest to His disciples (and us). That means His peace is legally ours. When we inherit a precious item, like a piece of jewelry from a beloved family member, that gift becomes lawfully ours. But it's up to us to accept and use the item. Otherwise, it sits in a drawer or closet untouched. How foolish we would be to inherit such a valuable gift like Christ's peace and allow it to go unused!

So we must not allow ourselves to be agitated and disturbed by all that is in this world: our problems, our commitments, or even the enemy of our soul. We cannot ever let ourselves be fearful or intimidated or unsettled. Jesus left His peace for our benefit, knowing all we would face and how desperately we would need it. When we feel fearful, we don't have to yield to fear. We can instead choose to make good use of the precious gift of peace that Jesus provided us.

Lord, thank You for bequeathing Your supernatural peace to me, leaving me with the priceless gift You knew I would need. When my heart begins to feel agitated, or I sense myself becoming unsettled or intimidated, prompt me by Your Spirit to stop myself from yielding to fear. Instead, help me accept Your peace and choose to regularly use and walk in what is legally mine. By Your Spirit, may I never permit my heart to be agitated or troubled, because Your supernatural peace is a priceless gift from You. Help me remember this and, despite all this world throws at me, use the peace You left me. In the strong name of Jesus, amen.

HEART NOTES

_____

_____

_____

_____

_____

38

Stand Your Ground

Put on God's complete armor, that you may be able to resist and stand your ground on the evil day [of danger], and, having done all [the crisis demands], to stand [firmly in your place].

EPHESIANS 6:13 AMPC

There are times we must stand our ground, resisting the enemy's taunts and lies and the confusion that creates knots in our hearts. This is only possible when we're equipped with the spiritual armor that God offers, which includes the belt of truth, the helmet of salvation, and the breastplate of righteousness. Wearing spiritual armor protects us in multiple ways: It prevents us from believing and yielding to the enemy's lies; it helps us stand firm in the truth of who we are instead of sinking into shame; it endows us with clarity of mind so we can discern the right way to go. Essentially, the magnificent armor God provides covers us, equips us, and enables us to stand firm.

Thus equipped, we are equal to every task. We can absolutely do all that our situation or crisis requires, because God supplies all we need to stand. But we must first put on the armor. It does no good to leave it leaning up against a wall or stored in a back closet. Through faith we wear it, and it enables us to stand our ground instead of sinking into despair. It helps us fight against discouragement and panic. It helps us continue to stand firm. We do not give up and we do not give in, but through His mighty armor we resist every evil effort. We stand, and we keep standing.

Lord, help me recognize my need for Your full armor and, by faith, apply it thoughtfully each day so I can resist the enemy's taunts and lies. Thank You that the armor You provide covers me and equips me so I am equal to every situation. I do not have to allow my heart to be pummeled, and I do not have to allow my mind to absorb every rogue hit, because Your armor covers and protects me. Give me the wisdom and grace to walk while wearing Your complete armor. Thank You that through Your divine provision I am equipped to resist every lie and scheme, to stand my ground and keep standing, and to walk in truth, faith, and peace. In Jesus's name, amen.

HEART NOTES

_____

_____

_____

_____

_____

39

A Holy Hideaway

> He who dwells in the secret place of the Most High
> shall remain stable and fixed under the shadow of
> the Almighty [Whose power no foe can withstand].
>
> **PSALM 91:1** AMPC

Where we live matters. Not only house-wise, but heart-wise. We can live in fear. We can live in denial. We can live in aggravation. We can live in regret. Each of these "places" creates tension and, if we continue to dwell there, leaves us feeling dissatisfied, isolated, unstable, or fearful. They're not wise, healthy places to hang out and call home; our hearts cannot thrive there.

But when we choose to dwell, abide, and remain in the secret place of the Most High—our private space with the Lord—we are stabilized and protected in a powerful way. When our "living space" is near the Lord, and He likewise lives in us, our lives are marked by peace. Ephesians 3:17 says, "Christ will make his home in your hearts as you trust in him. Your roots will grow down into God's love and keep you strong." Strong roots hold our hearts firmly in place.

The secret place is where only we and God go. It's here that the Lord invites our hearts. It's here that we can dwell because in His shadow we are utterly safe. It is our private place, secluded and intimate. It is the place our hearts hide in Him, and it is where we discover unfathomable peace. No foe can enter here, in this safe, peace-filled space—our holy hideaway.

Lord, help me not live in fear, denial, aggravation, regret, or anywhere else my heart cannot thrive. I do not want to dwell in places that make me feel insecure or weak or anxious. I want to dwell with You, in the secret place of the Most High, where my heart can flourish. Thank You that as I develop deep roots in Christ and live in this place close to You, my heart is stable and at ease because You are my foundation. God, draw me often to this place. Help me stay here with ever greater frequency, where no foe can enter. As I choose to dwell in the holy hideaway of Your presence, fill me with Your deep and abiding peace. In the precious name of Jesus, amen.

HEART NOTES

_____

_____

_____

_____

_____

40

Following the Spirit

Letting your sinful nature control your mind
leads to death. But letting the Spirit control
your mind leads to life and peace.

ROMANS 8:6

There's a tug-of-war being fought in most of our minds on any given day, and the easy way is not necessarily the right way. It is easy to think critical, negative, or fearful thoughts. When our sinful nature controls our minds, it is easy to entertain the bad, which causes a downward spiral in our souls that leads to the enemy's accusations and our own misery.

Essentially, our flesh and the Spirit are antagonistic toward each other. Galatians 5:17 says, "The sinful nature wants to do evil, which is just the opposite of what the Spirit wants. And the Spirit gives us desires that are the opposite of what the sinful nature desires. These two forces are constantly fighting each other, so you are not free to carry out your good intentions."

Learning to allow the Holy Spirit to control our minds takes practice, but through prayer and God's grace, we can pursue holy change. We can train our minds to follow the Spirit instead of being bossed around by anxiety or fear or negativity (or anything else). And when the Holy Spirit controls our minds, everything changes. Our very thoughts can then usher in sweet life and beautiful peace.

> *Lord, thank You for helping me recognize the tug-of-war in my mind. Help me not allow myself to go the easy, negative way. Help me not entertain and focus on the bad but instead learn to allow Your Holy Spirit to guide and control my mind, steering my thoughts toward all that is good and noble and excellent. Though my flesh and Your Spirit are antagonistic toward each other, teach me to daily surrender to You. May my thoughts be more frequently and more consistently directed by Your Spirit so that being led by You is the most natural thing for me. Thank You for always leading me into truth by Your Spirit. May I embrace and follow Your Spirit so I walk unswervingly in life and peace in Christ. In His awesome name, amen.*

HEART NOTES

_____

_____

_____

_____

_____

41

God Cares

I will be glad and rejoice in your unfailing love,
for you have seen my troubles,
and you care about the anguish of my soul.

PSALM 31:7

There's nothing we experience that escapes the Lord's notice. When troubles bring heaviness to our souls, He knows. When we're overwhelmed, uneasy, and anxious, He sees. He notes our troubles and understands our aching hearts. He sees all that brings disappointment and recognizes our inner pain. He is aware of our current fears and our desperate need for peace.

And the Lord cares. Deeply. Our hearts can take great comfort in knowing that our Creator cares about our most distressing situations. He sees all we endure and, in His great compassion, He empathizes. Hebrews 4:15 says, "This High Priest of ours understands our weaknesses, for he faced all of the same testings we do, yet he did not sin." This is how He understands our pain. He, too, endured testings, betrayal, grief, and pain—so He empathizes with us. God is not a distant, uncaring deity, but a loving heavenly Father who cares about the anguish of our souls.

Our hearts can be reassured that we do not walk through

our troubles and concerns alone. On the contrary, God remains unwaveringly near us. He is deeply concerned about all we're going through, daily offering us His comfort, empathy, and peace. In our Savior's unfailing love He cares about us, loves us, faithfully watches over us, and offers us His limitless grace—and because of that, we can rejoice and be glad.

Lord, I'm grateful that You see and understand everything that troubles me and causes internal upset. Not a single concern or situation in my life escapes Your notice. You know when I'm struggling, when I worry, and when anxiety squeezes my heart. Thank You for caring about the anguish of my soul. I'm grateful that You see all I endure and offer me comfort, empathy, and peace. Thank You that I am never alone. Thank You for comforting me and being with me and for teaching me to rest in Your unfailing love. In Jesus's name, amen.

HEART NOTES

_____

_____

_____

_____

_____

42

Matchless Companionship

The LORD longs to be gracious to you;
therefore he will rise up to show you compassion.
For the LORD is a God of justice.
Blessed are all who wait for him!

ISAIAH 30:18 NIV

What an astonishing thought—God desires to be merciful to us; He longs to be gracious to us. Our sovereign, holy God watches for opportunities to be good to us. Not because we are perfect. Not because we deserve it. But because God's very nature is generous and compassionate and kind, and He loves us with an everlasting love (Jeremiah 31:3). Our hearts can bask in the peaceful reassurance of His affection for us and His desire to bless us.

Our goal? To earnestly wait for Him despite the busyness of our lives and our long to-do lists. This is an inward anticipation our hearts can cultivate. We can long for and expect God's reassuring, calming presence in our daily lives—which pleases the Lord. In the middle of all that causes anxiety in us, we can still inwardly focus on and yearn for Him. He then pours out His favor, love, joy, and peace, reviving and delighting us with His matchless, unbroken companionship. We are blessed when we wait for Him, expecting Him to intervene in areas that concern us and anticipating His comfort and soft, gentle voice.

Lord, give me a heart that yearns for You and waits for You—for Your calming and satisfying presence. My heart swells with joy that You desire to be merciful and gracious to me, and I treasure the many blessings You give me. Thank You that despite my shortcomings and imperfections You pursue me with Your kindness and love. Please teach me to cultivate a desire for You, expecting Your very real presence in my daily life. Give me grace to sincerely wait on You and anticipate You. May my heart rest in the beautiful, peaceful reassurance of Your matchless, unbroken companionship. In Jesus's name, amen.

HEART NOTES

_____

_____

_____

_____

_____

43

Perfect Peace

You will keep in perfect peace
all who trust in you,
all whose thoughts are fixed on you!

ISAIAH 26:3

Perfect peace—that for which our anxious hearts yearn. We crave peace. We long for it. And yet, somehow, we tend to allow worry to step between us and peace. We permit this rude interruption when we obsess over unpleasant or disappointing circumstances. Or when we refuse to drop a matter, harping on it (even to ourselves) for hours—or days. All this focusing on our worries reminds us of our problems, which magnifies anxious thoughts and steals our peace. Jesus understands our human tendencies and challenges us: "Can all your worries add a single moment to your life?" (Matthew 6:27).

No, actually, they can't.

But what a difference we experience when we steer our thoughts away from our worries and instead consider God's promises. When we think about His blessings and align our hearts with the truth of Scripture, we experience peace. It requires serious effort on our part, but if we stop allowing ourselves to rehearse our current troubling situation, focusing instead on the One who *is* our peace, the atmosphere of our hearts changes from agitated to calm. As we fix our minds on the Lord and His truth, we can lift our worries and entrust them entirely into His capable, loving hands. As we choose to let go of worry and instead trust in Him, He promises to keep us in perfect peace.

Lord, my heart longs for Your peace. Please help me recognize when I need to redirect my thoughts from the issues that bring anxiety and point them back toward You. I surrender the circumstances that concern me to You. Lord, I trust You. Teach me to depend on You and keep my thoughts fixed on You, moment by moment when necessary. May my focus shift toward Your promises and blessings, and may my heart be realigned to the truth of Scripture instead of worry. As I lift every concern to You, may my focus shift toward all that You are because You are faithful and kind and good. Thank You for enabling me to redirect my thoughts. Thank You for calming my heart and filling me with Your perfect peace. In Jesus's name, amen.

HEART NOTES

_____

_____

_____

_____

_____

44

Flourishing

Dwell in Me, and I will dwell in you. [Live in Me, and I will
live in you.] Just as no branch can bear fruit of itself
without abiding in (being vitally united to) the vine,
neither can you bear fruit unless you abide in Me.

JOHN 15:4 AMPC

Not one of us is able to manufacture peace apart from Christ. Yet we often forget our need to remain near Him, overlooking the fact that apart from Him we cannot bear the fruit of peace (or any other fruit of the Spirit). For peace to flourish in our hearts, our hearts must first flourish in Jesus. Abide in Him. Dwell in Him. When we remain deeply connected to Jesus—through obeying Him, worshipping Him, reading Scripture, and praying—we dwell in Him. It's then that His peace permeates our hearts in a very real way because He is the Prince of Peace.

Apart from Christ we can do nothing (John 15:5). Our hearts wither and our peace evaporates. But when we are vitally united to Him, we will live rich lives and bear much fruit. We will be able to answer softly when a harsh word is spoken to us. We will love when it's not easy or convenient. Instead of holding a grudge, we will forgive. When we remain near Jesus, our anxiety levels naturally decrease, and we are filled with the precious peace we crave and He lavishly provides.

Lord, I sometimes forget how desperately I need to remain near You. Teach me to dwell in You at all times. May I always turn to You when a harsh word is spoken, when loving is not easy, and when it's hard to forgive. May my heart remain deeply connected to Yours so that I bear much good fruit, bringing honor and glory to the Father. May my heart flourish in You. May my anxiety levels decrease, and may Your peace in me increase and thrive. In the mighty name of Jesus, amen.

HEART NOTES

_____

_____

_____

_____

_____

45

Bubbling Hope

May the God of your hope so fill you with all joy and
peace in believing [through the experience of your
faith] that by the power of the Holy Spirit you may
abound and be overflowing (bubbling over) with hope.

ROMANS 15:13 AMPC

When we're tempted to feel hopeless because of a family member's stage 4 cancer diagnosis or our spouse's pornography addiction, we have an amazing God who understands, who never leaves us, and who is the source of our hope—the source of *all* hope.

Though we have a very real enemy who wants to strip us of hope—he'd love for us to completely let go of our hope, like a balloon released into the wind, never to be seen again—we can choose not to relinquish it. Our circumstances may be heartbreaking, but our hope is not in what we're facing. Our hope is in our faithful God's ability to intervene and in His offer of grace in the least likely of places. Our hope rests in God's power, His kindness, and His unfailing love. None of these disappear when we face painful situations. God is steadfast, and because He is the God of hope, we can always have hope.

When our hope collides with the unexpected and undesired, the Holy Spirit can help us hold on to our hope and multiply it so that it bubbles up in a refreshing, effervescent spring inside of us. This is what our awesome God offers: overflowing hope, supernatural joy, and unshakable peace in the unlikeliest places.

Lord, when my hope collides with the unexpected, help me know deep inside that You are now and will always be my treasured and secure source of hope. Help me not relinquish my hope but hold tight to it—and hold tight to You. God, You are able to intervene in every situation that concerns me. My hope is not in my circumstances but in You—in Your power, Your sovereignty, and Your ability. I'm grateful that no matter what I'm facing, You are able to multiply my hope, causing it to bubble up inside me like a refreshing spring when I need it most. As I continue to hope in You, fill me with Your supernatural peace. In Jesus's name, amen.

HEART NOTES

_____

_____

_____

_____

_____

46

Choose to Sing

As for me, I will sing about your power.
Each morning I will sing with joy about your
unfailing love. For you have been my refuge,
a place of safety when I am in distress.

PSALM 59:16

God's power and love are worth singing about, as the psalmist clearly reveals. When anxiety looms, we can set a fresh tone for our entire day with a song of gratitude. Worship changes the atmosphere of our hearts, reminds us of God's goodness, and fills us with His beautiful, refreshing joy. This telling verse reveals the psalmist's acute awareness of God's many blessings, such as His power at work in our lives, His love for us, which never ends, and the divine stability and peace He offers when our hearts are disturbed.

We can choose to sing when we're not feeling well, when we're so stressed we can't think straight, and when we're overwhelmed by the arduous season we're facing. We can choose to sing when we're feeling the pressure of an unflinching deadline, when we're late for a critical engagement, or when we're in serious personal distress. That sacrifice of praise not only pleases and honors God, but it also lifts our hearts.

Hebrews 13:15 encourages us to "offer through Jesus a

continual sacrifice of praise to God, proclaiming our allegiance to his name." Praising God helps us maintain divine perspective, prevents us from obsessing over what's in front of us, and keeps our eyes riveted on all that is eternal. Singing about God's attributes shifts our focus from all that makes us miserable to our King, who is the source of our solace, hope, and peace.

Lord, I want a heart that chooses to sing even when I feel overwhelmed with anxiety. Please give me grace to sing to You even when it is a sacrifice, because You are worthy of my praise. When I feel overwhelmed and beyond stressed, may my choice to praise You anyway honor You and draw me closer to You and set a beautiful new tone for the rest of my day. Teach me to sing more often and help me maintain an eternal perspective. Thank You for consistently being my refuge and safe place when my heart is distressed. Whatever I face, may a song be quick to erupt out of my mouth. Thank You for covering me with Your goodness, unfailing love, and peace as I sing. In the precious name of Jesus, amen.

HEART NOTES

_____

_____

_____

_____

47

Your Shield

The LORD is my strength and shield.
I trust him with all my heart.
He helps me, and my heart is filled with joy.
I burst out in songs of thanksgiving.

PSALM 28:7

There are days when we need serious help, days that take us by surprise, and days that threaten to suck the joy right out of us. Instead of allowing ourselves to fall into an ugly anxiety meltdown, we can pause, take a deep breath, and turn to our mighty God.

When our hearts are overwhelmed with fear or worry or anxious thoughts of any type, we can trust the Creator of the universe to guard and help us, especially when we're shaking on the inside. He Himself is our shield; we can duck behind Him while He deflects all the incoming attacks. On hard days we can entrust our worries to Him, releasing the weight of each one. He is also our strength; we don't have to be strong, because He is strong for us. We can rest in His abilities instead of trying to conjure up our own.

As the psalm points out, when we turn to God and trust Him, He helps us! *This* is how our hearts live at ease. *This* is when our hearts are filled with joy. *This* is why we are filled with thanksgiving and burst into song for our Savior.

Lord, when my days are long and hard, may my heart be quick to remember Your faithfulness to guard and help me. When everything in me wants to throw a fit or at least throw up my hands, may I choose to run to You and trust You. Help me lift everything that causes anxiety immediately to You and teach me to hide myself in Your shadow. Thank You for being my shield, for protecting me and deflecting the enemy's blows. Thank You for being strong on my behalf. Oh Lord, my heart is thankful for all You do for me, for all You are to me. May songs of praise well up from deep inside me. In Jesus's name, amen.

HEART NOTES

_____

_____

_____

_____

_____

48

God Gives You Rest

The Lord said, My Presence shall go
with you, and I will give you rest.

EXODUS 33:14 AMPC

It's easy to get swept up in the busyness of our many obligations and commitments, rushing through our days to make a dent in our lengthy to-do lists. When we feel the pressure to accomplish more than Superwoman could probably conquer (and she wouldn't have our time constraints either), we would do well to remember two things: In the middle of our crazy-busy lives, God's presence changes everything; and He offers us the rest we desperately need.

We can invite the Lord's presence through prayer or praise. A simple, "Lord, be with me," opens the door of our heart to Him. God's presence transforms us, strengthens us, and empowers us. It is in His presence that our hearts can rest, even when our days are nonstop. Even when obligations leave us stressed and exhausted. As we go about our daily lives, we can rest from striving, rest from anxiety, and rest from all worry. We can allow our minds to rest from the tension of trying to figure it all out.

Let's take a deep breath and, with holy determination, make it our goal to rest daily in God's love, His kindness, and His ability to faithfully and thoroughly handle every issue that concerns us.

Lord, as I go about the busy and sometimes frantic moments of my daily life, help me never move without You. Please put it in my heart to invite You daily to help me and be with me. Lord, I need You. I long for Your soul-transforming presence. I'm grateful that Your presence covers me, changes me, strengthens me, and equips me. I choose right now to make it my holy goal to rest in Your presence, because You are my solid Rock—You are everything to me. When my to-do list feels like more than I can manage, help me cease striving, worrying, and trying to figure everything out. Thank You that Your presence supplies me with grace for even the most overwhelming days. Thank You, Lord, for teaching my soul to rest in You. In Jesus's name, amen.

HEART NOTES

_____

_____

_____

_____

_____

49

Higher Things

Set your minds and keep them set on
what is above (the higher things), not on
the things that are on the earth.

COLOSSIANS 3:2 AMPC

et's face it. We live on planet Earth, and much of what consumes our thoughts involves our portion of this terrestrial sphere. Those weeds need to be yanked out of the dirt. Those emails require responses. And our dog needs a walk (pronto!). And then there are thoughts that disturb us. *What if they don't accept my apology? What if I can't bounce back from this injury? What if my house is broken into like theirs was?* In a single day our minds can consider hundreds of thoughts. If we're not careful, those disturbing reflections can ricochet around our brains and interfere with our peace.

Instead of allowing our minds to obsess over worries that provoke fear and anxiety, what if we—through prayerful recognition—took control of our thoughts and changed them? When we redirect our minds, we help our hearts remain calm. When we consider our many blessings, God's goodness and kindness toward us, and His love at work in our lives, we are actually setting our minds on things above. Compulsively focusing on negative issues, many of which we are powerless to change, only drags down our hearts. Redirecting our minds keeps us in an emotionally healthy place of light and truth. It brings our hearts into alignment with the Lord's, and that is where our joy and peace will thrive.

Lord, help me not fixate on disturbing thoughts that generate unnecessary anxiety in my heart. Prompt me by Your Spirit to recognize when my mind is heading the wrong way, and give me grace to redirect my thoughts and set my mind on higher things—such as Your goodness and kindness to me and Your unfailing love at work in my life. Help me resist compulsively focusing on the negative and instead turn my mind to light and truth. Teach me to cultivate gratitude and an awareness that what I think about matters. May my mind consistently focus on what pleases You and helps me. In Jesus's name, amen.

HEART NOTES

_____

_____

_____

_____

_____

50

An Open Heart

May He grant you out of the rich treasury of His
glory to be strengthened and reinforced with mighty
power in the inner man by the [Holy] Spirit [Himself
indwelling your innermost being and personality].

EPHESIANS 3:16 AMPC

There are places of our hearts that are open, where we allow many people access. And there are places we wisely guard from all except a trusted few—the places where confidential thoughts and desires exist. And then there are the secret areas of our heart that no one knows except us.

This secret place is the area where we must choose to allow the Lord access. He longs for us to invite Him into this precious, private space, because God Himself wants to dwell in the deepest part of our hearts. It is there, in the places we conceal from others, that He does His deepest work, pouring out of the treasury of His heart right into ours. This is where authentic renewal happens, and it is by His Spirit dwelling there that our hearts are transformed.

God Himself strengthens and reinforces our inner selves, making our hearts more like His. It is by His Spirit that we are bolstered with His unwavering stability. It is by His Spirit that anxiety's grip is loosened from our souls. And it is by His Spirit that our innermost beings are filled with unfathomable peace.

Lord, may my heart be ever open to Your Spirit, inviting and allowing You into the most private areas of my innermost being. Work in the deepest parts of my heart and bring transformation as only You can. Displace all anxiety and bring holy change by indwelling my innermost being. Reinforce me with Your mighty strength so that my heart and mind do not waver. Enable me to be stable in all I do. By Your Spirit may anxiety's grip on me be loosened from my soul. Make my heart more like Yours and fill me with Your supernatural peace. In the mighty name of Jesus, amen.

HEART NOTES

_____

_____

_____

_____

_____

51

Lean on the King

Those who trust in, lean on, and confidently hope
in the Lord are like Mount Zion, which cannot be
moved but abides and stands fast forever.

PSALM 125:1 AMPC

We have a very real enemy whose goal is to move us from calm to frantic, confident to shaky, peaceful to anxious. But we have a mighty God who is far greater, who desires to stabilize us when our hearts begin to tremble and fill us with His abiding peace. On days when we've had far too little sleep, we feel emotionally unsettled, or we simply seem "off," we do not have to allow ourselves to be pushed into a meltdown. Through Christ it is possible to retain our emotional and spiritual equilibrium, standing securely in Him.

The key to possessing an unshakable heart is knowing where (and upon whom) to lean. Trusting in people—even trustworthy loved ones—invariably leads to disappointment. We discover that mere humans are no adequate foundation. But we can trust in our kind and understanding and perfect God. Our hearts can fully lean on Him, wholly resting there. We do this through prayer and focusing on His faithfulness and power, which far surpasses the enemy's schemes or our own insecurities. He is our steadfast foundation, the One in whom we can confidently hope. When our hearts cling to Him we won't be easily moved; our awesome King enables us to stand, unshakable.

Lord, I long to possess an unshakable heart. When the enemy is pushing hard and my own inadequacies bubble up, help me not allow myself to be moved from peace to anxiety. Teach me to stand securely in Christ. Help me trust You and lean on You, Lord, because Your power is far superior to my own weaknesses or anything the enemy attempts. However I'm feeling, may I consistently trust and believe Your Word, knowing that You are the One who stabilizes my heart and gives me peace. Thank You for being my firm support, my eternal Rock. In Jesus's awesome name, amen.

HEART NOTES

_____

_____

_____

_____

_____

52

Sheltered

I will say of the Lord, He is my Refuge and
my Fortress, my God; on Him I lean and
rely, and in Him I [confidently] trust!

PSALM 91:2 AMPC

There are times our hearts desperately need relief, a break from both inner and outer pressures. We may feel overwhelmed by our own expectations, or we may feel like failures as we face a new challenge. Or perhaps we feel stressed by our jobs, a rough season in our marriage, or formidable personal goals. Whatever the sources of our agitation, there exists a beautiful refuge where we can decompress and experience God's love and peace.

A refuge is a trusted place of safety and security where we are sheltered from all danger and trouble. It is a place in which our hearts can relax and be at ease. God Himself is this place for us. He is our sanctuary, our protection, our holy reprieve. Because God is faithful and all-powerful, we can allow ourselves to lean on Him when we are overwhelmed and weary. We can pause and breathe deeply, getting a mental and emotional break from every source of pressure, knowing He loves and understands us. When we're battling worry or stress or anxiety, we can confidently rely on and hide ourselves in Him, our refuge and fortress.

Lord, thank You that whether I feel overwhelmed or inadequate or like I'm hanging by a thread, You offer me beautiful rest. Whatever specific inner or outer issue I'm battling, You are my consistent place of safety and security. You are my sanctuary and protection. In You I am sheltered from the dangers of discouragement, anxiety, and stress. When my heart is overwhelmed, teach me to run to You and lean on You, resting my mind and emotions in the fortress of Your loving and capable care. You are faithful, and I can always rely on You and trust You, my Prince of Peace. In Jesus's name, amen.

HEART NOTES

_____

_____

_____

_____

_____

53

Resisting Panic

Be strong and courageous! Do not be afraid
and do not panic before them. For the LORD
your God will personally go ahead of you. He
will neither fail you nor abandon you.

DEUTERONOMY 31:6

t is tempting (and completely natural) to shift into panic mode
when we are hit with unexpected troubles, when what is in
front of us startles us, or when our hearts become fearful. When
we receive a call from our son or daughter telling us they've been
in a car accident, of course our heart rates double. If we discover our much-loved pet has days to live, how could we not
be upset? When our boss informs us of a pay cut, it's normal to
feel alarmed. And yet, God reminds us that we do not have to
panic. He encourages us to be strong and courageous. We don't
have to allow fear to control us or steal our peace.

How? How do we battle the anxiety that frequently wells up
in our hearts? By remembering who God is: kind, mighty, and
all-powerful. He loves us and watches over us with tender care.
Psalm 121:5 says, "The LORD himself watches over you! The
LORD stands beside you as your protective shade." He is near
us and with us, and we resist upset by remaining near Him. By
trusting Him. By knowing He is faithful.

We also resist panic by breathing in this truth: The Lord Himself goes before us, and He will not abandon us. What a great, reassuring comfort! God is with us. Always. As we consider these priceless facts, may our hearts remain calm, stable, and at ease. He is sovereign over all that makes us fearful or overwhelmed.

Lord, when I'm faced with the unexpected and feel upset and frightened, will You please help me remember who You are? Help me recall that You are kind and mighty and all-powerful. My heart is so grateful that You watch over me with tender care. May I always walk in peace, choosing not to panic because You are sovereign and trustworthy, and through You I really can be strong and courageous. Thank You for reassuring my heart, reminding me that You go ahead of me and You absolutely will not fail or abandon me. My heart takes immense comfort in Your steady, ongoing faithfulness. In the strong name of Jesus, amen.

HEART NOTES

_____

_____

_____

_____

_____

54

Entering Sacred Rest

We see that they were not able to enter [into His rest],
because of their unwillingness to adhere to and trust
in and rely on God [unbelief had shut them out].

HEBREWS 3:19 AMPC

There is a beautiful place of rest in Christ that we must make every effort to enter. We must not permit our doubts to keep us from it. We must not be reluctant to trust the Lord with the issues that most disturb our hearts. When Moses led the Israelites out of Egyptian slavery, many were unwilling to trust and believe God. Sadly, their unbelief shut them out of the very place for which their hearts yearned. We, too, must guard against an unwilling heart, because unbelief kept the Israelites from the land of Canaan, which God had vowed to give them—and we also long for a promised land of rest.

Our willingness to believe and trust God takes us to a place of abiding rest. The place where we no longer strive. The place where we find relief from the weariness of trying to control everything because we completely trust and depend on Him instead of ourselves.

As we believe the Lord through faith, confident that He is our source and surrendering ourselves afresh to Him as many times as it takes, our hearts can rest in serene contentment. This place of absolute trust and reliance on Him is our true place of sacred rest.

Lord, my heart yearns for rest in You. Help me guard against an unwilling heart. Teach me to believe You, trust You, and depend on You in ever-increasing measure. May doubt and my own human efforts never prevent me from entering Your rest. May my faith increase as I choose to rely on You no matter my circumstances. Fill me with Your hope and peace and lead me into this sacred place of divine rest in Christ. May my heart always believe, always seek, and always trust You. In Jesus's precious name, amen.

HEART NOTES

_____

_____

_____

_____

_____

55

On Guard

Be on guard. Stand firm in the faith.
Be courageous. Be strong.

1 CORINTHIANS 16:13

When anxious thoughts and emotions float toward our brains like so much negative dust swirling through the air, we do not have to allow them to land on us. We can be alert and guard ourselves. In fact, we absolutely must.

Through discernment, we can learn to distinguish all that does not align with truth and all that steals our peace—whether that is our own negative inner commentary, the critical accusations of the enemy, or even doubt or confusion that randomly hits us. As we pay attention and pray, we can trust that God is with us, helping us notice and resist all such mental and emotional opposition. This is how we remain on guard.

We stand firm in our faith by familiarizing ourselves with Scripture and the Lord's faithfulness and by recognizing all He has already done for us and through us. Through His Word we also discover His perfect character; we learn how very dependable He is and discover His limitless power and unfailing love. We see how well He knows us and loves us (Psalm 139:1; Jeremiah 31:3). We grow to understand that through Him we absolutely can be courageous and strong because we can do all things through Christ who strengthens us (Philippians 4:13).

Aligning our hearts with these truths (and so many others) helps us live brave, faith-filled lives. Knowing our Lord Jesus more deeply and accurately transforms our hearts, helps us live out today's key verse, and enables us to walk in His abiding peace.

Lord, please teach me to recognize and be on guard against all that steals my peace. I don't want to automatically allow anxious thoughts and emotions to enter into and influence my mind and heart. Give me grace to notice thoughts that don't align with truth so I can resist and refute all that would harm my joy and well-being. Help me stand firm in my faith, knowing You love me, cherish me, and are with me. Fill me with courage and help me be brave and strong. Thank You for Your limitless power and unfailing love at work in my life. May I consistently stand firm in my faith, walking in Your deep, abiding peace. In the name of the Prince of Peace, Jesus, amen.

HEART NOTES

_____

_____

_____

_____

56

Reassurance

Don't be afraid, for I am with you.
Don't be discouraged, for I am your God.
I will strengthen you and help you.
I will hold you up with my victorious right hand.

ISAIAH 41:10

The enemy wants us to live fearful and discouraged lives. And honestly, some days that's far too easy to do. Our lives aren't always neat and tidy; there's much we don't understand. Even a single glance at news headlines can make our hearts cringe. But we don't have to sink down into discouragement, even when fear hits hard and we're seriously tempted to go there. We have a choice, because when we turn to Almighty God, "whose power no foe can withstand" (Psalm 91:1 AMPC), He strengthens and helps us. He is good, forgiving, merciful, loving, compassionate, and all-powerful. He is the One who upholds us, who keeps us from going under, who prevents our hearts from sinking.

We don't have to be afraid, because God is with us. When all appears hopeless and our anxiety levels climb to ceiling level, we can remember who our God is: victorious and mighty, our "ever-present help in trouble" (Psalm 46:1 NIV).

Let's pause and absorb these amazing facts, allowing them

to settle deep into our hearts. The enemy is no match for the Lord. God Himself holds us up with His strong right hand. We don't ever have to be afraid because He lifts us, encourages us, and is always with us.

Lord, though there is much I don't understand, You are good and You are mighty. You are my strength and my source of joy, and I will not give in to the enemy's schemes or yield to fear and discouragement. I will cling to You, my faithful, mighty God. Regardless of what I'm facing, may my heart be strengthened and encouraged by You. You are the One who upholds me with Your victorious right hand. You are the One who strengthens and helps me. I will not be afraid or discouraged, because You are my God. Thank You for helping me remember who You are: You are good and merciful, forgiving and all-powerful. Thank You for fortifying and reassuring and permeating my heart with Your peace. In the matchless name of Jesus, amen.

HEART NOTES

57

Every Comfort

Blessed be the God and Father of our Lord
Jesus Christ, the Father of sympathy (pity and
mercy) and the God [Who is the Source] of every
comfort (consolation and encouragement).

2 CORINTHIANS 1:3 AMPC

Our good heavenly Father is aware when we endure rough
days and especially challenging periods. He sees and
comprehends all we go through, but He doesn't stop there.
He is the Father of sympathy. In fact, God can sympathize
because He became a man, as Hebrews 4:15 makes clear. "This
High Priest of ours understands our weaknesses, for he faced
all of the same testings we do, yet he did not sin." This means
the Lord understands us on a deep and personal level because
He also endured extreme hardship, rejection, and betrayal (to
name just a few of the Lord's bitter experiences). This is how
He can empathize and offer our hearts comfort unlike anyone
else. He understands us because He was one of us.

God's heart feels for us, and in His great mercy He offers us
His warm comfort. He is the source of *every* comfort. Through
Him, our hearts are supported and encouraged. In the middle
of all we're going through, we can breathe in His soothing presence and peace and experience His consolation.

Lord, I'm grateful that You are aware of all the rough days and challenges I'm currently experiencing—and the ones on my horizon. You know and understand and comprehend all I go through because You also lived in this sin-sick world, enduring hardships I can scarcely imagine. Just that fact is a huge comfort to me. You are my good heavenly Father, the Father of sympathy. You understand me and completely know my pain. More than that, You are merciful and sympathetic. Thank You for reaching out and comforting my heart right when I need it. Thank You for consoling and encouraging me through Your comfort. I will let my heart rest in You and breathe in Your soothing presence. In Jesus's name, amen.

HEART NOTES

_____

_____

_____

_____

_____

58

Not Alarmed

They all saw Him and were agitated (troubled
and filled with fear and dread). But immediately
He talked with them and said, Take heart!
I Aᴍ! Stop being alarmed and afraid.

MARK 6:50 AMPC

There are times that, like the disciples in a storm-tossed boat, our hearts are alarmed by the gale around us. We cry out, but when Jesus appears and does what we do not expect or acts in a manner different from what we anticipated, our human minds simply cannot fathom what He is doing. Then our hearts totter and become fearful. *What's happening, Jesus? Why aren't You doing what I thought You would do?* We waver between trust and angst. We may sense He is near, but when things don't unfold the way we hope or desire, we become fretful, dreading what might happen next.

But Jesus understands when we do not. He recognizes when we are troubled and dread overtakes us. And He whispers what we desperately need to remember: "Take heart! I Aᴍ!" Immanuel, God with us, is comfortingly close (Isaiah 7:14). In other words, we aren't alone. However wild the winds, He never leaves us or forsakes us (Hebrews 13:5). He is with us in the storms, anchoring our hearts, soothing our nerves, and establishing His plans and purposes in us, for us, and through us. He is sovereign, and He is in control. We do not have to be alarmed or afraid. Jesus Himself is with us.

Lord, I confess that there are times I waver between trust and fear because I simply do not understand what You are doing. Will You please help me have faith in You anyway? However agitated my heart may feel, help me not be alarmed or afraid. I am grateful that when fear attempts to overtake me, You are there. I am never alone because You never leave me. You are sovereign and in control, and I do not have to be upset or afraid. Thank You for filling my heart with courage and peace. I choose to trust You, Lord Jesus, I AM, my Prince of Peace. In Your name, amen.

HEART NOTES

_____

_____

_____

_____

_____

59

God Speaks Peace

I listen carefully to what God the Lord is saying,
for he speaks peace to his faithful people.

PSALM 85:8

t is so important that we make time to learn and even cherish Scripture. It is tempting to think that we do not have time or that the Word doesn't apply to us or that we can't understand what it says, but through Scripture our eyes are opened. Psalm 119:18 says, "Open my eyes to see the wonderful truths in your instructions." As we learn God's many promises, we discover hope and gain clarity and insight. We realize that Scripture isn't dormant, but very much a living thing.

Hebrews 4:12 says, "The word of God is alive and powerful. It is sharper than the sharpest two-edged sword, cutting between soul and spirit, between joint and marrow. It exposes our innermost thoughts and desires." This mean God's Word lives and moves *in us*, accomplishing the very purposes for which it was sent (Isaiah 55:11). And through it we learn God's character and become familiar with His voice. We discover that God is worth listening to above all other voices. His voice is at once comforting, enlightening, and assuring. It brings clarity and encouragement to our hearts. Above all, when we learn to love Scripture and listen carefully for God's voice through it, He speaks peace to our hearts.

Lord, please give me not only a deep love for Scripture but also the desire to spend time in it and learn more of it. Open my eyes to the wonderful truths in Your Word. Teach me to recognize Your still, small voice, discerning it more clearly and accurately. Help me listen carefully for You, knowing that You can give me ears to hear what Your Spirit says. Thank You for speaking peace over my heart, mind, and life through Scripture. May I daily choose to make time to read and cherish Your Word. Thank You for speaking personal, meaningful words to me, words that fill my soul with Your amazing peace. In Jesus's name, amen.

HEART NOTES

_____

_____

_____

_____

_____

60

A Brave Life

> God has not given us a spirit of fear and timidity,
> but of power, love, and self-discipline.

2 TIMOTHY 1:7

Fear can get stirred up through many means, including past experiences, concern about the future, insecurity, or an overly active mind. But fear does not come from God. We do not have to yield to it, entertain it, or allow it to influence us. Fear interferes with our lives, enticing us to entertain worst-case scenarios and making our hearts insecure and timid. Fear can hinder us from that confrontational conversation, stop us from taking the next God-orchestrated step, and make us miserable with anxiety.

But the Lord offers us far better resources that help us live brave lives: power, love, and self-discipline. His unlimited power equips us with all we need for each situation. Philippians 4:13 (AMPC) says "I am ready for anything and equal to anything through Him Who infuses inner strength into me." Next, God's awesome love never fails (1 Corinthians 13:8). "God *is* love" (1 John 4:8, emphasis mine), and His unfailing love working in us and through us is greater than fear. Self-discipline is one of the fruits of the Spirit ("self-control" in Galatians 5:23) that helps us resist giving in to fear. When we resist fear's tactics and employ these gifts, we can experience less fear and live brave.

Lord, whenever fear disturbs my heart, may I instantly recognize it and refuse to entertain it or yield to it. Teach me not to allow fear to influence me or stop me, knowing that fear is never from You. Help me instead embrace the wise choices that will help me live a brave life through Your unlimited power, Your unfailing love, and self-discipline. May fear have no hold on me. May my heart be strong, bold, and very courageous, today and always. In the strong name of Jesus, amen.

HEART NOTES

_____

_____

_____

_____

_____

61

Cheering Your Soul

In the multitude of my [anxious] thoughts within me,
Your comforts cheer and delight my soul!

PSALM 94:19 AMPC

Even the psalmist dealt with anxious thoughts. Plenty of them, apparently. And so it is with us. We wrestle with various and ongoing unpleasant thoughts due to factors we cannot control, sometimes even struggling with ridiculous worst-case scenarios concocted by our nervous, overactive minds. *What if this happens? What if that doesn't work out? Why did I even think I could handle this big change?* Anxious thoughts somehow multiply in our brains, tumbling over each other, making our hearts uneasy and keeping us awake at night.

And yet, God Himself—the ultimate comforter—steps into the melee of our minds, completely changing the atmosphere because He is light and love. When we pray, He hears us, and darkness flees. First John 1:5 says, "This is the message we heard from Jesus and now declare to you: God is light, and there is no darkness in him at all." Instead of allowing anxious thoughts to torment us and deprive us of sleep, we can lift every issue to the Lord, asking Him to help us, intervene in our circumstances, and fill us with His peace. He will! The Lord uplifts our hearts with His joy, bringing vibrant gladness to our souls.

Lord, You see the many anxious thoughts I wrestle with, including the ones that keep me up at night. You know where my mind sometimes dwells. There is much I cannot control and much I struggle with internally. I invite You to intervene in the situations that concern me; I lift each one to You, entrusting it into Your sovereign care. Please step into all that is going on inside me, my good heavenly Father. Displace darkness and bring peace. Bring the reassurance that Your comforting presence offers. Change the atmosphere of my heart with Your light, Your truth, Your joy, and Your peace. Fill my heart with cheer, delight my soul, and bring Your vibrant gladness to my life. In the awesome name of Jesus, amen.

HEART NOTES

62

Rooted in Love

Christ will make his home in your hearts as
you trust in him. Your roots will grow down
into God's love and keep you strong.

EPHESIANS 3:17

Jesus, who walked this earth and had no place to lay His
head, wants to make our hearts His permanent residence.
He wants us to be so comfortable and at ease with Him that He
can dwell within us and make the changes He desires.

That's a good thing, because we all need God to transform
our hearts. This happens by faith as we make room for Jesus in
our everyday lives. We do this through spending time with Him
daily, listening for His voice, worshipping Him, and reading
His Word. We do this by asking Him to keep our hearts in tune
with His so that our days and even our thoughts are directed by
Him. We do this by asking Him to give us ears that hear what
His Spirit is saying so we can recognize His still, small voice. We
do this by obeying His voice, even when it's out of our comfort
zone or just plain hard to do so.

As our hearts accommodate and welcome the Prince of
Peace, we become more and more deeply rooted in His unfailing love. This helps us to rest secure in Him. His love grounds
us, stabilizing our emotions and easing our inner lives. As Jesus

lives in us, we live in Him, and this changes everything—it changes us.

Lord, I'm grateful that Your permanent residence is inside me. It is there You can make the changes I so desperately need. It is there I can flourish because You work deep within me. It is there I am secure and thriving, rooted deep in Your unfailing love. Teach me to spend time with You daily, keeping my heart in tune with Yours and hearing what Your Spirit is saying to me. Teach me to recognize Your voice and give me great grace to obey You. Thank You, Jesus, Prince of Peace, for transforming my anxious heart into a peace-filled heart. As You dwell in me, I am rooted and stable and secure in You. You change absolutely everything. In Your name, amen.

HEART NOTES

_____

_____

_____

_____

_____

63

Filled with Love

May you experience the love of Christ, though
it is too great to understand fully. Then you
will be made complete with all the fullness
of life and power that comes from God.

EPHESIANS 3:19

How imperative it is to know and experience the reality of
Christ's love! We must not shortchange ourselves, only
hearing about or holding a vague idea of this divine love. The
apostle Paul understood how vital it is for every believer to go
beyond the basic knowledge of God's love, imploring us to
experience it for ourselves.

We experience God's love when we linger over and inhale
Scripture, allowing it to stir our hearts and believing what it says.
(When was the last time a verse made us cry?) We experience
His love when we sense His very real presence through prayer.
(When was the last time we did not rush into and out of our
prayer time?) We experience His love when we adhere to truth
and do what the Bible says, like choosing to forgive. Then His
amazing peace rushes into our hearts. (When was the last time
we quickly let go of a stinging offense?)

Although Paul points out that the love of Christ is too great
to fully understand, when we ask God to allow us to experience

His love for ourselves, it touches His heart—and He will begin that process in us. He longs to reveal Himself to us so we can experience Christ's love in a deeper way. If we will allow it, God's love will fill our entire being with the richness of His presence. We will be utterly transformed as we are flooded with God, who *is* love (1 John 4:16).

Lord, I long to experience the reality of Your great love for myself. My heart is open to You. Teach me to linger over Scripture, allowing it to touch my heart deeply. Help me not rush into and out of times of prayer with You. Help me adhere to Your truth, doing what it says, however hard that may be. Please enable me, by the power of Your Spirit, to know and experience the love of Christ for myself—practically, intimately, and daily. May Your unfailing love fill my entire being, transforming me, softening me, and changing my heart. Fill me with the richness of Your solid, comforting, assuring presence. Fill me with Your love. In the awesome name of Jesus, amen.

HEART NOTES

_____

_____

_____

_____

64

The Spirit-Infused Life

I say, walk and live [habitually] in the [Holy] Spirit
[responsive to and controlled and guided by the Spirit];
then you will certainly not gratify the cravings and
desires of the flesh (of human nature without God).

GALATIANS 5:16 AMPC

We can cultivate the habit of walking and living in the Holy Spirit, encouraging our hearts and minds to respond more to Him than to anyone or anything else. When we're tempted to respond in anger or fear, we can instead, by His power at work in us, respond more appropriately. But this takes practice and commitment. When we yield our minds to the Holy Spirit, we are far less likely to indulge in snarky comebacks, yell at the person who just cut us off in traffic, or completely stress out.

We also need to walk in the fruits of the Spirit, described in Galatians 5:22-23: "The Holy Spirit produces this kind of fruit in our lives: love, joy, peace, patience, kindness, goodness, faithfulness, gentleness, and self-control." The degree to which we are abiding in Christ and allowing His Spirit to develop this fruit, guiding and controlling us, is the degree to which we are living in the Spirit.

Our human nature can be ugly. But through God's guidance and our willingness to live in the Spirit, we learn not to gratify our flesh but instead to behave more like Him—living vibrant, Spirit-infused lives.

Lord, please help me commit to, practice, and cultivate the habit of walking in the Holy Spirit. Help me develop the fruit of the Spirit, daily striving to yield to Your Spirit at work in me and to produce fruit that honors You and blesses those around me. Teach me to yield my mind to You, allowing myself to be controlled and guided by Your Spirit instead of allowing my flesh and emotions to boss me around. Thank You for enabling me to be far more responsive to Your Spirit than to the desires of my own flesh. May I yield more to Your Spirit than anyone or anything else. In Jesus's name, amen.

HEART NOTES

_____

_____

_____

_____

_____

65

Big, Beautiful Places

He brought me forth also into a large place;
He was delivering me because He was
pleased with me and delighted in me.

PSALM 18:19 AMPC

An anxious heart is a severely restricted heart. And yet, God has so much more for us. He knows when we're hemmed in and constrained by anxiety, fear, worry, or anything else. Through Christ He releases us into the beauty and freedom of His wide-open spaces of heart freedom—so that instead of feeling crushed by anxious thoughts, we can experience the relief of His abundant peace. It's sort of like when we take a long, uphill walk on a hot, humid day. Soon we're miserably overheated, our faces beet red, our clothes clinging to our sweaty selves. And then we get to jump into a big, sparkling, refreshing swimming pool.

In our distress we can call on the Lord, and He hears us (Psalm 18:6). He rescues us from all that overwhelms us, lifting us out of the stifling anxiety that has enclosed our hearts and into His remarkable, tranquil, and reviving presence. Our heavenly Father understands us and takes pleasure in us, just as we are. What a stunning thought! He loves us and frees our hearts, leading us toward refreshing joy and peace in Christ.

Lord, You see and understand my heart. You know where I am hemmed in and confined by anxiety and fear and worry and all the other stresses that pile up inside me. And yet, God, You do not leave me there. When I'm distressed and call on You, You hear and rescue me, leading me out of the stifling enclosure of anxiety. You escort me into Your very presence, filling me with Your remarkable, refreshing presence. Thank You for displacing every trace of anxiety with Your very real peace. Teach me to walk daily in the freedom of Your refreshing joy and tranquility. In Jesus's name, amen.

HEART NOTES

_____

_____

_____

_____

66

Rewarded

I will cry to God Most High,
Who performs on my behalf and rewards me
[Who brings to pass His purposes for
me and surely completes them]!

PSALM 57:2 AMPC

What a relief—not everything in our world is up to us. Not the serious issues that stir crankiness and short, tight breaths. Not the disappointments that make our hearts ache. Not the hopes we're still longing to see fulfilled. Thankfully, God knows our weaknesses and steps into the areas where we need Him, whether it's the heavy loads we're attempting to carry or the inner places in which we strongly desire transformation.

God knows our frail nature and how much we need His help. Like a parent with a small child who struggles to put away her toys on the highest, unreachable shelf, God sees our efforts and limitations and swoops in to help us. He does what we cannot do. It is because of Him that we experience change, relief, freedom, and peace.

When faced with our own inadequacies and inabilities, all we have to do is cry for God, who intervenes on our behalf and rewards us by faithfully accomplishing His plans for us, completing each one. He is so faithful. So kind. So powerful. What a reassuring, beautiful relief.

Lord, I am beyond relieved that not everything is up to me. I take great comfort in knowing that when my life feels far too heavy a load to bear, I can cry out to You. When I long for encouragement and transformation and help, You faithfully and powerfully step in. When my assurance is evaporating, You offer fresh hope. You always hear me, You know how desperately I need You, and You go one step further to perform on my behalf, accomplishing what I never could. When I am not up to the task and my best efforts are inadequate, I'm grateful that You know my areas of weakness and are my strength, rewarding me by bringing to pass Your plans and purposes for me. In the awesome name of Jesus, amen.

HEART NOTES

_____

_____

_____

_____

_____

67

Empowered

He gives power to the faint and weary, and to
him who has no might He increases strength
[causing it to multiply and making it to abound].

ISAIAH 40:29 AMPC

There are days and seasons when our ability to endure and "just keep going" seriously dwindles, our efforts leave us exhausted, and our worries leave us depleted. We're only human, and at a certain point we each discover that our own strength only gets us so far. And yet, our faithful Creator, who knows our limitations, gives power to us—the faint and weary. How reassuring!

When our entire being needs recharging, we must turn to the right place—Jesus. Ephesians 6:10 (AMPC) tells us, "Be strong in the Lord [be empowered through your union with Him]; draw your strength from Him [that strength which His boundless might provides]." This means that rather than attempting to manufacture our own vigor, we must recognize our source and remain connected to Him.

When our capacity diminishes, His is just getting started. God strengthens us supernaturally, multiplying His power at work in us so that, like the story of the loaves and fish (see Mark 6:30-44), our little becomes much. When we are near Him, our

Almighty God multiplies our efforts and our strength. Through Him, our weary hearts are replenished, refreshed, and empowered.

Lord, when I feel weak and weary, my heart is overwhelmed, and I am at the point of anxious exhaustion, will You please refresh me with Your power? When I am depleted by all my efforts and have no strength, Lord, You can increase my strength and give me the ability to keep going. My power may be limited, but Your power has no limits. You multiply my efforts, making them abound. Thank You for strengthening my heart, mind, and physical body. Thank You for replenishing me with Your power and causing my peace and strength to flourish as only You can. In Jesus's name, amen.

HEART NOTES

_____

_____

_____

_____

_____

68

Unquestionably Free

The Lord is the Spirit, and wherever the
Spirit of the Lord is, there is freedom.

2 CORINTHIANS 3:17

We do not have to allow ourselves to be bombarded by rogue emotions, inner chaos, or insecurity. Whether our responses arise from a person's unkind comments, uncertainty concerning chronic health issues, or wanting to feel like we belong in a new neighborhood, they don't have to control or overwhelm us. Instead of permitting our peace to be choked off by such unwelcome events, we can turn to the Lord, who offers freedom. We can pray, asking Him for insight and discernment, grace to forgive, and healing and courage. He always hears us, and it is His delight to encourage our hearts and answer us.

The Holy Spirit offers freedom from all that oppresses and disturbs us. He displaces darkness and guides us into all truth (John 16:13). He is a freedom-giving Spirit, and when we allow Him access to every area of our lives, every section of our minds and hearts, and every dark corner, He liberates us from all that is not of Him. John 8:36 (AMPC) says it beautifully: "If the Son liberates you [makes you free men], then you are really and unquestionably free." May He give us great grace to invite Him into every area of our lives and walk in ever-increasing freedom.

Lord, help me not allow myself to be jerked around by rogue emotions, inner chaos, or insecurity. Give me discernment to recognize when my peace is being hampered or stolen and help me turn to You. Lord, You know the specific areas where I need freedom, so please move in me. Search out every area and target oppression of any kind. Free my heart. Free my mind. Free my emotions. I invite You into every area of my life so Your beautiful Spirit can bring ever-increasing freedom. Thank You for giving me insight and grace and healing and courage. Thank You for liberating me so I am really and unquestionably free. In the awesome name of Jesus, amen.

HEART NOTES

_____

_____

_____

_____

_____

69

Soul Rest

Come to Me, all you who labor and are heavy-laden
and overburdened, and I will cause you to rest. [I
will ease and relieve and refresh your souls.]

MATTHEW 11:28 AMPC

What a compelling invitation from Jesus. Few of us do
not labor under weighty loads. Few of us do not have
heavy hearts. We've experienced loss, grief, failures, and obsta-
cles. We've lived through trauma, illness, distress, and heart-
break. We languish under oppression.

And yet, Jesus's three words extend to us the hope that it
does not have to remain this way: *Come to Me.*

This requires action on our part—a choice to turn from all
that overwhelms us and toward Him. We come to the Lord by
quieting our hearts through prayer and worship. Sometimes
we come to the Lord by sitting quietly in His presence. And
He offers us beautiful respite and deep relief. His warm words
coax our weary selves toward exactly what we need: soul rest.
He longs to lift all the heaviness from our shoulders and hearts.

Psalm 55:22 (AMPC) tells us to "cast your burden on the
Lord [releasing the weight of it] and He will sustain you." When
we come to Him and relinquish our loads, releasing each one
into His loving and capable hands, He relieves our hearts from

every burden. He refreshes our souls. He enables us to rest in Him, reviving us and filling us with His peace.

Lord, when I am exhausted by my heavy loads and overwhelmed by all I'm attempting to deal with, help me remember that this is not the way You intend for me to live. Help me simply turn my heart away from all that overwhelms me and come to You, relinquishing every burden to You. Thank You for offering me the relief and rest my soul desperately needs. Thank You for easing my heart and relieving me of every weight. Thank You for refreshing my weary soul, reviving my heart, and sustaining me with Your peace. In Your precious name, amen.

HEART NOTES

_____

_____

_____

_____

_____

70

What You Cannot See

We fix our eyes not on what is seen, but
on what is unseen, since what is seen is
temporary, but what is unseen is eternal.

2 CORINTHIANS 4:18 NIV

We get it so wrong. What we see, the issues right in front of us, are typically what we think about and consider most. Yet the things upon which we fixate—the real matters causing angst and discouragement in our souls—are only temporary. This is why we must, by God's grace, begin to develop an eternal perspective.

As 1 Corinthians 13:12 (KJV) tells us, "We see through a glass, darkly." This means that, like looking into a foggy mirror, our perception is distorted and incomplete. God sees the complete picture; we don't. Our understanding this side of heaven is limited, and what we *do* see isn't always an accurate reflection. Yet we should not stumble about in dark anxiety of soul. Instead, we must learn to fix our eyes on unseen things, such as faith, hope, and love—and even God Himself, who is Spirit (John 4:24). This is how we begin to focus on what is eternal.

Through faith we believe that God is at work behind the scenes despite how things appear. Through hope we resist discouragement and stand with persevering hearts. Through love our hearts are softened, and we are transformed into God's image. May He give us grace to live with an eternal perspective, approaching every day like truly wise people who see beyond what is in front of us.

Lord, sometimes I get so caught up in the issues in front of me and so busy with the things of life that I forget to keep an eternal perspective. Help me remember that everything around me is temporary—but You, God, are eternal. Help me develop an eternal perspective, not by ignoring what concerns me, but by remembering that what I see is temporary. Help me fix my eyes on what is unseen, and in so doing remain focused on You, because everything else on this earth— all that I see—is foggy and distorted. Help me concern myself with the things that matter most to You. Captivate my heart, Lord, and help me live like a wise person who sees beyond what is in front of me. In Jesus's name, amen.

HEART NOTES

_____

_____

_____

_____

_____

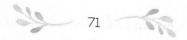

71

Reservoirs of Strength

Those who trust in the LORD will find new strength.
They will soar high on wings like eagles.
They will run and not grow weary.
They will walk and not faint.

ISAIAH 40:31

There are vast reservoirs of strength available for those who refuse to trust in their own power but choose instead to trust in the Lord. Our worst days, our deepest fatigue, our absolute exhaustion is no hindrance for the Lord, who graciously says to us, "My grace is all you need. My power works best in weakness" (2 Corinthians 12:9). When our anxious hearts convince us that we cannot possibly meet with that person or answer that awkward phone call, His power meets us and equips us. Like a refreshing stream it rushes in, filling every gap, more than making up for what we lack.

When we trust God despite what we're facing, we discover fresh strength. When we trust His power to be more than adequate to cover our physical and mental limitations on any particular day, He enables us to soar above every heavy hindrance. His strength far surpasses our human constraints, allowing us to achieve far more than we could on even our best day. And even on our weariest day, through His power we can persevere, because He endows us with fresh fortitude.

Lord, help me not trust in my own frail abilities, but instead trust You. Thank You for filling me with new strength—Your limitless strength. When I feel weary and exhausted physically or mentally or spiritually, may I consistently believe You, trust You, and hope in You. Because You are my strength, my glory, and the lifter of my head, help me soar over everything that attempts to weigh me down. Equip me by Your effusive grace and enable me to run without weariness. Help me trust You for fresh strength, believing Your power is more than adequate to cover my limitations. Armed with that power, may I accomplish all You lead me to do, without giving up or giving in. In the mighty name of Jesus, amen.

HEART NOTES

_____

_____

_____

_____

_____

72

Led by the Spirit

Those who are dominated by the sinful nature think about sinful things, but those who are controlled by the Holy Spirit think about things that please the Spirit.

ROMANS 8:5

t is simple, really: Our sinful nature is bossy and domineering. It wants to control us through unholy thoughts and, through our weak human flesh, steer us down dark roads that lead nowhere good. It's through sinful thoughts that we end up convinced we will never win over anxiety. Or we end up mercilessly comparing ourselves to someone and then cringing with insecurity. Sinful thoughts also lead us to hold a serious grudge.

But how different our thoughts are when the Holy Spirit controls us. We develop healthy, holy thinking. We learn to recognize and embrace truth—*I really can do everything through Christ who strengthens me* (Philippians 4:13). We learn to discern and refute lies—*I won't think the worst of them; I'll give them the benefit of the doubt* (1 Corinthians 13:7). We come to understand and truly believe that God is for us and not against us (Romans 8:31).

Led by the Spirit we think about things that please Him. Compelled by His gracious kindness and wisdom, our thoughts lead to the pursuit of all that gratifies God—which leads us to good, vibrant, light-filled places.

> *Lord, help me resist my bossy flesh and the unholy thoughts that lead to fear, worry, discouragement, and anxiety. In the name of Jesus, I refuse to go in that direction or allow such feelings to dominate me. Instead, I will yield my thoughts to You. May Your Holy Spirit lead me and teach me to think about things that please You. Cover my mind and guide not only my thoughts, but my entire life. By Your Spirit, help me recognize and embrace truth, discern and resist lies, and develop healthy, holy thinking. As I yield my mind to You, point my thoughts toward all that is good and right and peaceful. In Jesus's name, amen.*

HEART NOTES

_____

_____

_____

_____

_____

73

Shield of Love

You bless the godly, O Lord;
you surround them with your shield of love.

PSALM 5:12

There are days when a shield would come in handy—providing protection from negative words, unpleasant confrontations, strife, or bad news. Though God doesn't hand us a physical piece of armor to lug around, He blesses us by surrounding us with His shield of love. Because love never fails (1 Corinthians 13:8 NIV), we know it's always there, staunchly guarding us day in and day out. Because God *is* love (1 John 4:8), we understand that the Lord Himself surrounds us.

What a comfort to know He constantly remains near. That means even on our worst days, when we can scarcely crawl out of bed, His great love shields us from discouragement and despair. It means when our to-do list is longer than our arm, His love shields us from the lie that we can't possibly manage it all. And it means when we must confront a friend in love, our nerves and fear don't have to get the best of us. God's supernatural covering provides ample grace for everything we face. His love is always there, reassuring us, accepting us, cherishing us, and inviting us toward Him. It is always there. Like an invisible defense system, His love encircles us, covers us, and brings encouragement to our hearts.

Lord, You are the King of my heart. You are gracious and generous, blessing me and providing all that I need—going so far as to cover me with Your shield of love. Nothing can penetrate it because You encircle me and conceal me. I'm grateful that Your unfailing love guards me day in and day out, cherishing me and reassuring me. Thank You for surrounding me with Your presence, protecting me from discouragement, worry, stress, or anything else that stokes anxiety in me. Thank You for surrounding me with an amazing shield of love. In Jesus's name, amen.

HEART NOTES

_____

_____

_____

_____

_____

74

Breathing Space

He makes me lie down in [fresh, tender] green pastures;
He leads me beside the still and restful waters.

PSALM 23:2 AMPC

God knows when our hearts, minds, and physical bodies need rest, even when we don't recognize it ourselves. When we crowd too many commitments onto our calendar and struggle with exhaustion, depriving ourselves of much-needed margin, He sees. He knows that we are mere humans who sometimes ignore our need for respite. And because He knows us so intimately, down to the number of hairs on our heads (Luke 12:7), He understands precisely when we need a break.

So He leads us exactly where we need to be. If we are wise, we won't resist when He offers us beautiful places of rest in Him. Places where our hearts can lie down and be nurtured and tended to and refreshed by the One who made them. Places where our souls can be still. Places where we can indulge in a holy pause and just be. When life becomes frantic and we are frazzled, we don't have to continue until we fall down. We don't have to resist taking a much-needed mental, spiritual, or physical break. We can find divine breathing space. God beckons us toward lovely waters of rest, where His peace washes over us and revives us.

Lord, thank You for not only providing my sometimes frantic and frazzled heart a place of respite and peace in the middle of the craziness of everyday life, but for being the place to which I can run. Lord, You are my source of peace. You provide beautiful places of rest for my soul. When my heart, mind, and body are overwhelmed, "I cry to you for help…Lead me to the towering rock of safety," as Psalm 61:2 says. Thank You for refreshing and rejuvenating me when life chips hard at my heart. Thank You, Jesus, that You lead me to this place where I can be still and You can restore my soul. In Your beautiful name, amen.

HEART NOTES

_____

_____

_____

_____

_____

75

Reliable Help

God is our refuge and strength,
always ready to help in times of trouble.
So we will not fear when earthquakes come
and the mountains crumble into the sea.

PSALM 46:1-2

Some seasons of our lives are far more difficult than others. Some periods of anxiety are far more intense. And some days feel three and a half years long. This is precisely when we must rush into our good heavenly Father's presence. He knows the season we're experiencing. He knows our hearts, understands us, and fiercely loves us. In times of extreme distress, He is a sheltering stronghold to which we can continually resort (Psalm 71:3). Our hearts can relax and be at ease just knowing He—our steadfast fortress—stands ready to shelter us.

Regardless of the level of hardship we're experiencing, our faithful God is always ready to help—always. We do not have to stress out, panic, or fear, because He Himself is our utterly dependable refuge and strength. However arduous our days or weeks, God is our Rock in whom we find protection (Psalm 18:2). He is reliable and always prepared to assist, relieve, and comfort our quaking, overburdened hearts. Because He is always ready to aid us, we never have to feel alone. He is there, arms outstretched, ready to welcome us into His embrace.

Lord, You are so good! I'm grateful that You know me, understand me, and fiercely love me. You are my consistent, reliable help when life is hard, when anxiety is intense, and when my days seem far too long. Help me breathe in this truth and run to You, my fortress and protection. Thank You for being my steadfast refuge and strength in times of trouble, my solid Rock. Help me not panic or fear, because You are always ready to help me. Hold my heart continually in Your peace as I look to You and completely entrust every care into Your faithful hands. Thank You for relieving and comforting my heart. In Jesus's name, amen.

HEART NOTES

_____

_____

_____

_____

_____

76

Two Simple Choices

Don't be afraid; just believe.

MARK 5:36 NIV

Jesus knows that we struggle with fears and worries and anxieties. He knows our hearts. He knows we are frail humans, often subject to our own rogue emotions and circumstances beyond our control. He understands when our overstimulated brains won't shut down. He perceives when our minds relive an upsetting incident over and over. He knows that fear and anxiety crash into our faith, making it hard to believe Him.

When the apostle Peter dared to step out of the boat (see Matthew 14:28-33), he began to sink because he feared the wind and waves. Aren't we the same? We attempt to be brave, but then surges of angst knock us off balance, and we sink.

And yet, with deliberate brevity, Jesus gives two simple instructions in Mark 5:36: "Don't be afraid. Just believe." This is exactly what our anxious hearts need to hear. The Lord invites us to resist fear and believe Him over all the anxiety-producing events we're experiencing. It's an irresistible invitation that lovingly reminds us who He is: He is greater than our storms; He is our steadfast, water-walking help; and He is in the wind and waves with us. Jesus is our Prince of Peace. He beckons us, asking us to leave fear behind and trust Him. May we choose to say in faith, "Lord, I will not be afraid. I will believe."

Lord, when fear and anxiety crash into my faith and I am afraid, help me run to You and follow Your two simple instructions. Teach me to remember that You are greater than all my fears. Thank You that when my emotions go crazy, You are the stabilizing force right beside me, greater than every storm, and You are good. I believe, Jesus, that You are greater than all the upheaval in my heart. I believe that You can deal with all that concerns me. I believe that You are the Prince of Peace. Thank You for calming my heart and helping me always accept Your loving invitation. In Your name, amen.

HEART NOTES

_____

_____

_____

_____

_____

77

Be Still

Be still in the presence of the LORD,
and wait patiently for him to act.

PSALM 37:7

Instead of allowing ourselves to become anxious and upset because our child continues to fight an illness...or to stew in our concern about ongoing marriage issues...or to worry ourselves sick because we apologized to a friend weeks ago but silence painfully ensues...what if we stilled our hearts and asked God to give us His extraordinary peace while we wait for our hoped-for results? Instead of feeling frustrated, what if we allowed ourselves to sit in the Lord's presence and trust Him?

Yes, waiting is hard. It's no one's favorite thing. Yet what we consider to be inconvenient delays often hold divine purpose. For instance, during divine delays we can learn to trust God more and depend on Him in a deeper way. We can also learn to rest more instead of trying to push our agenda, which causes our faith to increase.

Training ourselves to be still is challenging. But when we refuse to allow our hearts to grow anxious and instead embrace holy stillness, focusing on God's faithfulness, we mature, grow in grace, and demonstrate our confidence in God. By His grace, we can rest in His faithfulness, kindness, and goodness. We really can be still and wait patiently for Him to act.

Lord, when I am tempted to allow all I am waiting for to make me upset or anxious, help me instead be still in Your presence. As I wait on You, may my faith increase. As I trust You for answers that have not yet come, fill me with Your peace. I'm grateful that what appears to be an inconvenient delay can hold divine purpose, so please help me learn. Teach me to depend more on You. May this be a time I mature in Christ, and may my heart choose to believe as I wait and trust You more. In the precious name of Jesus, amen.

HEART NOTES

_____

_____

_____

_____

_____

78

The Mind of Christ

We have the mind of Christ (the Messiah) and do hold
the thoughts (feelings and purposes) of His heart.

1 CORINTHIANS 2:16 AMPC

We would be wise to consider the power of our minds and thoughts and where they can take us. They can take us to good or bad places, peaceful or stressed-out places. When we allow ourselves to dwell on negative thoughts, our hearts spiral. When we focus on our fears, they unfortunately flourish right before our overactive brains.

Yet, Scripture declares that when we belong to Jesus, we have the mind of Christ. In other words, knowing Him should radically alter the very way we think. Jesus is the Word made flesh (John 1:14). When we allow His Spirit to fill and control us, our thoughts and feelings and purposes will begin to align with His heart and with Scripture, which is truth.

Romans 12:2 says we should "let God transform you into a new person by changing the way you think." This is how transformation happens: by allowing Scripture and the Spirit of the Lord to infiltrate our thought process, challenge us, point out erroneous thoughts, and help us recognize and align ourselves with truth. Possessing the mind of Christ enables us to think more clearly and accurately. It displaces worry and stress and always fills our minds and hearts with His amazing peace.

Lord, help me always be aware of where my mind and thoughts are taking me. Help me not allow my thoughts to take me to bad, negative, stressed-out places. May I not pursue or entertain negative thoughts that create stress and anxiety in my heart. Right now I choose to align my mind with Yours, Jesus. Thank You that because I am a new creation I do have the mind of Christ. Thank You that as I read Your Word I am actually transformed and my mind is renewed. May my thoughts consistently align with what is true, honorable, right, pure, lovely, admirable, excellent, and worthy of praise, as Philippians 4:8 reminds me. May Your Spirit influence my mind and bring my heart into alignment with Your feelings and purposes. Fill my mind and heart with Your amazing light and truth and peace. In Jesus's name, amen.

HEART NOTES

_____

_____

_____

_____

_____

79

All You Need

Your heavenly Father already knows all your needs.
Seek the Kingdom of God above all else, and live
righteously, and he will give you everything you need.

MATTHEW 6:32-33

We are seriously needy people. A plethora of physical, emotional, and material needs mark our lives. There are days that our bodies ache, times when our hearts hurt, and seasons of emotional turmoil. Then there are bills to be paid and obligations we must meet. Our needs this side of eternity vary but never end, and yet these verses tell us that our needs cannot be the primary focus of our lives.

We don't have to obsess over all our needs (thank God!) because our good and kind Father already knows each one. He understands all we must deal with and take care of. He cares about everything that concerns us, yet He encourages us to live beyond the temporal, keeping our focus on His kingdom. One of the ways we do this is by entrusting all our concerns to Him. Everything. This frees our hearts, helping us concentrate more on His kingdom and living righteously: keeping our spiritual ears tuned to Him, making time for reading Scripture, singing to Him, and praying.

When we seek God's kingdom first, we keep an eternal

perspective. We know Him and allow Him to lead and direct us. We entrust our every concern into His faithful hands. As we do this, God graciously gives us everything we need.

Lord, help me remember that You know the specifics of my every need, so I don't have to obsess over each one. Will you please give me grace to live beyond the temporal so that my life is more than rushing here and there? Help me trust You with everything that concerns me—all my physical, mental, and emotional needs. As I do, may I experience more heart freedom. May I live a righteous life marked by prayer, worship, and seeking Your voice. May my heart be consumed with all that matters to You. And may I always choose to seek Your kingdom first. In Jesus's awesome name, amen.

HEART NOTES

_____

_____

_____

_____

_____

80

The Battle Is God's

This is what the LORD says: Do not be afraid!
Don't be discouraged by this mighty army,
for the battle is not yours, but God's.

2 CHRONICLES 20:15

On extremely blustery days, stress, worry, and anxiety can seem like overwhelmingly strong, invincible enemies that never let up. It can feel as if the barrage of arrows hitting our hearts will never cease. It can seem like we will never win this battle. But those are lies.

The truth is we do not have to be afraid, because the Lord Himself fights for us. He is strong and mighty, so we don't have to fear. He is our hiding place, and in the thick of our most anxiety-producing battles we can run to Him. Psalm 91:2 says, "This I declare about the LORD: He alone is my refuge, my place of safety; he is my God, and I trust him."

Instead of yielding to fear and discouragement, we can trust that the Lord is on our side and willing to intervene. On difficult days our stance can be counterintuitive as we allow our hearts to rest in Him. Instead of hyperventilating we can expect Him to fight the battle for us. He will. It is not all up to us; the battle is not always ours, but it *is* always God's.

Lord, I'm grateful that even on my worst days—especially on my worst days—I do not have to give in to what feels like an army of fears and discouragements. Teach me to expect You to step in on my behalf. I'm grateful that this current battle and all that stokes anxiety within me is not left to me, because You fight for me. You are strong and mighty, and You are my place of safety. I will not hyperventilate. I will not take it all on myself. I will entrust my heart and all that concerns me to You. Thank You for being the safe refuge where I can dwell. Thank You for Your faithful love and for employing Your power and Your awesome, mighty ability on my behalf. In the strong name of Jesus, amen.

HEART NOTES

_____

_____

_____

_____

_____

81

Encouraging Words

Worry weighs a person down;
an encouraging word cheers a person up.

PROVERBS 12:25

Anxiety is like a colossal, wearisome chunk of granite lodged in our hearts; it weighs us down with its enormous heaviness. It chokes out our joy and squashes our peace. It stifles us and prevents us from moving forward. We were not meant to carry such an immense load.

When we sense such weight in our hearts, we would be wise to consider what we allow in. Are we believing lies? *I'm nowhere near smart enough. This situation is just never going to change.* Or are we entertaining doubts? *I'm not qualified, so I might as well not even try. Meeting them for lunch is way out of my comfort zone, so I'll just stay home instead.*

Wrestling with anxiety is already hard enough—why not reassure ourselves by speaking Scripture and other positive words that we desperately need to hear and will encourage our hearts instead of dragging them down? *I may feel inadequate, but I will "be strong in the Lord and in his mighty power"* (Ephesians 6:10). Or, *I'm so weary, but "he gives power to the faint, and to him who has no might he increases strength"* (Isaiah 40:29 ESV).

Proverbs 25:11 says, "A word fitly spoken and in due season

is like apples of gold in settings of silver" (AMPC). Words are powerful. They can lift us up, revive our hearts, and give us the encouragement we need to keep going.

Lord, when anxiety weights down my heart, please give me wisdom and discernment not to believe lies or entertain doubts that accumulate inside and drag me down. Teach me to engage in positive self-talk by speaking Scripture and other life-giving words to myself. When I need to be lifted up, will You please send encouraging words to me? May I be quick to encourage myself and others with words of kindness. And may my heart be open and receptive to the various forms of encouragement You send my way. Thank You, Lord, for filling my heart and mind with Your joy, presence, and peace. In Jesus's precious name, amen.

HEART NOTES

_____

_____

_____

_____

_____

82

The Rock Beneath Your Feet

Truly my soul finds rest in God;
my salvation comes from him.
Truly he is my rock and my salvation;
he is my fortress, I will never be shaken.

PSALM 62:1-2 NIV

ncomparable soul rest happens when we step close to God. When anxiety steals our breath, we can simply turn away from the crazy, turn toward Him, and allow ourselves to be still in His sweet presence. Near Him our souls can breathe, soothed and comforted by our good heavenly Father. However fierce the storm around us, our hearts can cry out to Him, "Be to me a rock of refuge in which to dwell, and a sheltering stronghold to which I may continually resort" (Psalm 71:3 AMPC). He is the beautiful, secure place where we can always stand. The place where we are always safe. The place where our hearts can experience reprieve and peace.

On bad days when we're feeling inexplicably edgy or just off-kilter, when our pulse is far too high and our spirits far too low, He steadies and calms our hearts. God is our trustworthy fortress—the safe, inviting place where our weary hearts can always take refuge. Near Him our hearts are safe and our emotions are calmed. Because He is the solid, stabilizing Rock beneath our feet, we need never be shaken.

Lord, I'm grateful that even in the middle of flat-out awful days, my soul can find incomparable, soothing rest as I stand in You. In my worst moments help me run to You, my sheltering stronghold, my safe place. Stabilize and calm my heart and emotions. May Your very real presence cover me, and may my heart always find refuge in You, my fortress. Thank You for being the rock beneath my feet and the God in whom I confidently trust, so that I am never shaken. In the strong name of Jesus, amen.

HEART NOTES

_____

_____

_____

_____

_____

83

Reviving Promises

Your promise revives me;
it comforts me in all my troubles.

PSALM 119:50

Occasionally we wake up and, instead of feeling bright and cheerful, our hearts feel heavy. Maybe we feel overwhelmed by a new project on which we're embarking. Maybe we've received a *no* when we seriously longed for a *yes*. Maybe we've prayed for an open door, and yet doors have remained closed. Feeling upset, disappointed, and frustrated can make our hearts feel oppressed. But instead of taking stock of all that stirs angst in our souls, what if we steered our hearts toward God's promises?

The good news is that God whispers unique, personal promises to each of us. How encouraged our hearts would be if we took time to remember them, focusing on them instead of our problems! God also gives specific promises through His Word. When our hearts are troubled and in desperate need of assurance, all His promises offer comfort and bring hope. Through Scripture, God promises us many good things, such as peace (John 14:27), joy (John 15:11), and the comforting fact that He will never leave us (Hebrews 13:5). Every promise from the Lord brings soul-reviving assurance to our troubled hearts. When we write them down, remember them, and focus on them, they lift us, reminding us of God's goodness and His faithfulness.

Lord, thank You for the specific promises You have whispered to me. Help me remember each one and hold fast to them, for You are good and faithful and kind, and I believe that Your plans for me will surely prevail. When my troubled heart begins to wilt, may Your promises always console me, comfort me, and fill me with the holy hope that is offered through Your Word. I'm determined to hold tightly to Your every promise and to discover fresh promises through Scripture, knowing You are sovereign and able. Through Your Word I am greatly encouraged. Thank You for all Your promises for my life, for they revive me. In Jesus's name, amen.

HEART NOTES

_____

_____

_____

_____

_____

84

Equal to Anything

I have strength for all things in Christ Who empowers
me [I am ready for anything and equal to anything
through Him Who infuses inner strength into
me; I am self-sufficient in Christ's sufficiency].

PHILIPPIANS 4:13 AMPC

Few things cause as much apprehension as feeling un-
equipped to handle the tasks and problems before us. In
our natural humanity, we feel weak and ill equipped. Maybe
you've had thoughts like these: *I'm supposed to do what? There's
just no way that can happen; I'm not prepared! I couldn't possibly
tell them that; they'll never believe me!*

And yet, even when we are absolutely certain that we *could
never,* here's something to consider: God does not leave us
stranded in our human weakness. In other words, we don't
attempt our tasks and deal with our problems on our own—
He helps us. Thank God! Through Christ, we are empowered
with all we need. He gives us insight, courage, wisdom, and the
skill and ability to navigate everything on our horizon.

Through Christ, we truly are equal to anything, not because
we've got it all together and are anxiety free, but because He
infuses us with inner strength. We are equipped by the King of
kings and the Lord of lords. It is His strength that enables us.

This is a beautiful truth: For every trial, every hardship, everything that makes us quiver on the inside, we are completely up to the task because of *God's* ability. He supernaturally equips us, and because of that, we are well able to face it all.

Lord, You see the tasks and issues before me, and You know how inadequate and ill equipped I feel concerning each one. God, I'm going to trust You to equip me with all I need through Christ. Thank You for making me ready for anything and equal to every situation because of Christ's strength. Thank You for His ability that flows through me, equipping me for every challenge I face. Thank You for giving me insight, wisdom, courage, and the skill and abilities I need. Thank You that I truly can do all things through Christ. Because You supernaturally equip me, I am well able to face what comes my way. In Your awesome name, amen.

HEART NOTES

_____

_____

_____

_____

_____

85

A Fresh Attitude

Be constantly renewed in the spirit of your mind
[having a fresh mental and spiritual attitude].

EPHESIANS 4:23 AMPC

Our minds are rather like water heaters. They can accumulate all sorts of gunk. That argument? Those unkind words? Those doubts and fears? They tend to accrue and sometimes even create bad attitudes. Those "sediments" interfere with proper function, making the mind work harder and burn out sooner. When hurts, doubts, disappointments, fears, and anxieties pile up, they "clog" our ability to keep our minds aligned with the truth.

This is why Scripture advises us to constantly renew our minds. We do this primarily through reading God's Word—which, as Hebrews 4:12 tells us, "is alive and powerful. It is sharper than the sharpest two-edged sword, cutting between soul and spirit, between joint and marrow. It exposes our innermost thoughts and desires." In other words, Scripture helps us see ourselves as we really are.

God's Word also has the power to change the way we think, and isn't that what we most need? Romans 12:2 says, "Don't copy the behavior and customs of this world, but let God transform you into a new person by changing the way you think." By reading Scripture, taking time to pray, and choosing to let go and forgive, we are constantly renewed in our minds, and our attitudes won't get in the way. This is how we keep our "water heater" minds clean and fresh and flowing properly. This is how we gain a fresh mental and spiritual attitude.

Lord, please help me not allow mental or emotional gunk to accumulate and clog my mind. Prompt me to recognize by Your Spirit when hurts, doubts, disappointments, fears, or anxieties begin to pile up. Help me choose forgiveness. Teach me to bring my mind into alignment with Yours, relinquishing every concern to You instead of allowing them to accrue. Help me make progress in these areas by regularly reading Your Word, spending time in vibrant prayer with You, and always being led by Your Spirit. By Your grace, help me develop and maintain a fresh attitude. In Jesus's name, amen.

HEART NOTES

_____

_____

_____

_____

_____

86

A New Focus

Letting your sinful nature control your mind
leads to death. But letting the Spirit control
your mind leads to life and peace.

ROMANS 8:6

Who—or what—controls our minds makes all the difference. There are thoughts that lead us to dark places, and there are thoughts that lead us straight toward the light. Becoming more aware of our thoughts and learning to recognize which way they are heading is the crucial first step toward a Spirit-led mind.

When our minds entertain critical, negative, dark thoughts, we spiral emotionally, and our peace completely evaporates. This happens when we give in to distorted thinking—such as, *My life is never going to change*, or, *Obviously they don't like me*. But we can stop allowing our negative, sinful nature to be in charge. It's a battle, but through prayer and awareness we can choose to challenge those distorted thoughts and then redirect them by allowing the Holy Spirit to lead our thinking. We can pause and ask Him to bring clarity and light to our minds.

And He will! He will teach us to resist the negative and think more accurately and in a healthy way. He always leads us toward life, joy, and peace. When we allow the Holy Spirit to lead our minds, we focus on truth, which fills our hearts with light.

Lord, please help me recognize when my thoughts are heading in the wrong direction. Help me not give in to distorted thinking, following after sinful, negative thoughts that cause me to spiral and lead me to dark places. Help me instead stop every thought that is not from You, redirecting my mind by Your grace. Help me choose life. Teach me to stop and ask You for clarity and light in my mind. Help me be consistently led by Your Spirit toward life, joy, truth, and peace. May I be drawn to You, and may my mind be unswervingly filled with and directed by Your beautiful Spirit. In the remarkable name of Jesus, amen.

HEART NOTES

_____

_____

_____

_____

_____

87

Shaking Off the Lies

Paul shook off the snake into the
fire and was unharmed.

ACTS 28:5

We must be careful and wise about what we allow to affect us. Too many times we accept negative thoughts about ourselves. Too often we believe and internalize harsh words or untrue accusations against us. Those words then burrow deep, inflicting pain and harm in our souls. The enemy wants to attach himself to us, injecting the venom of hurt, anger, upset, and stress straight into our hearts. John 10:10 reminds us that "the thief's purpose is to steal and kill and destroy."

But when the enemy strikes, what if we, like the apostle Paul, simply shake it off? Instead of accepting his lies and allowing hurts to deeply affect us, what if we say, "No, Satan, no"? This means that instead of coming into agreement with lies, we align ourselves with truth by reminding ourselves who we are. For starters, we are chosen (1 Thessalonians 1:4), loved with an everlasting love (Jeremiah 31:3), and victorious (Romans 8:37).

Instead of allowing hurts to affect us, what if we forgive, let them go, and shake off the enemy's attempts to harm us? What if we shake off every lie and go about our business—trusting

God, praying, singing, and walking in His amazing peace instead?

Lord, help me be prayerful and careful about what I allow into my heart. Teach me not to accept or believe or internalize any words that are harmful or untrue. When the enemy strikes, help me not allow the venom to take root. Help me forgive, let it go, shake it off, and go about my business, standing firm in my identity in Christ and trusting You to deal with the adversary. Instead of crumpling, simmering, or quaking, may my response to Satan's every attack be to resist and then pray, sing, and walk in Your peace. Help me remember that I am chosen, loved, and victorious. God, You are faithful and powerful and able to deal with the enemy as You enable me to hold on to my peace. Thank You, Lord. In Jesus's name, amen.

HEART NOTES

_____

_____

_____

_____

_____

88

A Happy Heart

A happy heart is good medicine
and a cheerful mind works healing,
but a broken spirit dries up the bones.

PROVERBS 17:22 AMPC

What price could we possibly place on a happy heart? Is it not a happy heart that enables us to endure life's difficulties? Is it not a happy heart that helps us deal with the hard moments of daily life, softening their incessant whine? In fact, a happy heart is like the best medicine currently available.

One of the ways we can cultivate a happy heart is through gratitude. Noticing and appreciating all God has given us and done for us displaces worry, agitation, turmoil, guilt, disappointment, and whatever else takes up too much room inside us. Celebrating our blessings lifts our hearts out of anxiety. Psalm 92:4 says, "You thrill me, LORD, with all you have done for me! I sing for joy because of what you have done." Now *that* sounds like a happy heart!

Likewise, a cheerful mind is itself healing, lightening our loads and transforming our perspective. We can see our circumstances through negative eyes or grateful eyes. We can focus on all our complaints, or we can take stock of what is good. May God give us grace to approach each day by choosing two things that make all the difference and bring beautiful healing: a happy heart and a cheerful mind.

Lord, will You please help me cultivate a grateful heart and see with grateful eyes? Teach me to notice and celebrate the many blessings You have given me. In the middle of my sometimes-overwhelming life, please give me grace to consistently live my days with a happy heart and a cheerful mind. I'm grateful that through this divine perspective anxiety is displaced and healing comes. I'm grateful that through Your joy my load is lightened, because Your joy is my strength, as Nehemiah 8:10 reminds me. In Jesus's name, amen.

HEART NOTES

_____

_____

_____

_____

_____

89

Minuscule Troubles, Eternal Splendor

Our light and momentary troubles are achieving for
us an eternal glory that far outweighs them all.

2 CORINTHIANS 4:17 NIV

Though often it does not feel like it, the hefty weight of our
troubles—the sicknesses, the accidents, the heartaches, and
the grief we experience here on earth—are minuscule compared
to the eternal splendor they are producing in us. That is why
the apostle Paul considered his troubles "light and momentary."
He understood that what we see and endure is temporary, and
what we cannot see is eternal (2 Corinthians 4:18).

This unfathomable, heavenly perspective came from the man
who five times endured thirty-nine lashes, three times was beaten,
once was stoned, three times was shipwrecked, faced various
dangers and hunger and cold, and much more (2 Corinthians
11:23-27). And yet he understood that these troubles were actually producing and achieving in him a holy, remarkable transformation. May God grant us this same perspective!

If we are willing to consider not only that our problems will
fade but also that they are accomplishing for us a vast and tran-
scendent glory, hope can flourish. We will understand that our

lives on this earth are not all there is and that the best truly is yet to come. Our faithful God knows and sees and understands what we're enduring and is using it all for His eternal purposes. A beautiful reward awaits us.

Lord, I confess that considering my troubles light and momentary is a challenge for me, particularly when anxiety hits my heart hard. Help me have an eternal approach, understanding that every one of my troubles are temporary and that You are at work even in my hardest moments, doing what only You can do: producing and achieving an eternal glory for me. May this fresh viewpoint strengthen me and boost my heart and mind. May it fill my heart with hope and peace. Thank You that all I'm enduring is truly temporary, that You are eternal and unchanging, and that You love me and are with me through it all. Fill me with courage and holy determination and the ability to live my life with this divine perspective. In the awesome name of Jesus, amen.

HEART NOTES

_____

_____

_____

_____

_____

90

Take Comfort

We take comfort and are encouraged and
confidently and boldly say, The Lord is my Helper;
I will not be seized with alarm [I will not fear or
dread or be terrified]. What can man do to me?

HEBREWS 13:6 AMPC

Even on our bleakest days, our hearts can be greatly assured and comforted when we hold the confident stance that the Lord is our helper. This means that even when an unexpected phone call brings bad news, we do not have to allow dread to overtake us. When we're assigned a distressing task, we absolutely do not have to allow our hearts to succumb to fear. Instead of being "seized with alarm," we can run to the Lord and allow our hearts to be reassured by Him, trusting that He is sovereign, He is for us, and He will help us.

Our hearts can rest in the heartening truth that God is with us and is greater than anything or anyone. This holy knowledge fills us with divine courage and unshakable peace. Whatever hits us, whatever scary or unpleasant facts we face, we can still be bold, encouraged, and confident because the Lord is our helper.

Psalm 28:7 reminds us, "The LORD is my strength and shield. I trust him with all my heart. He helps me, and my heart is filled with joy. I burst out in songs of thanksgiving." With joy-filled hearts we can sing, letting our hearts soar above our fears.

Lord, help me walk in boldness and confidence, absolutely convinced that You are my helper. Even on distressing days, may my heart be comforted and encouraged because You are faithful and kind and sovereign, and You are with me. Help me not succumb to fear or terror or any other form of anxiety. Help me walk in confident assurance, Lord, because You are my champion, my protector, and my defense. May this holy knowledge fill me with assurance, comfort, courage, and unshakable peace. Give me a joy-filled heart that sings to You and rises above my anxieties. In the strong name of Jesus, amen.

HEART NOTES

_____

_____

_____

_____

_____

91

Still Your Heart

Be still, and know that I am God!

PSALM 46:10

Our minds can easily slip into overdrive when we evaluate all the what-ifs, attempting to figure out every detail of our situations and obsessively calculating our next step. It's a temptation we face when we feel deeply concerned about the direction our life is going or when we aren't happy with our circumstances. Some of us are wired this way; we're natural overthinkers. Some of us indulge when we're feeling unusually apprehensive. Either way, this excessive mental activity takes a toll, feeding our worries and stirring up anxieties until our peace evaporates completely.

In the midst of this, God invites us to make a decision that goes against our instincts. When everything in us is whirling and calculating, He encourages us to be still, to step away from every worry and all our mental activity and know Him. Be with Him. Rest in Him. It's a bold step, but not as risky as it may seem, because "the LORD is merciful and compassionate, slow to get angry and filled with unfailing love" (Psalm 145:8).

Our hearts can truly rest in the Lord, knowing He is constantly at work so our minds don't have to be. Psalm 138:8 says,

"The LORD will work out his plans for my life—for your faithful love, O LORD, endures forever." When we still our hearts and minds, meditating on who God is and on all of His awe-inspiring qualities, our inner beings experience the relief of a quiet, peaceful heart.

Lord, I'm sensing that I need to stop all my mental activity—worry, anxiety, fear, obsessing over the what-ifs—and just be still. God, everything in me wants to work it out or else stress out, but instead I am going to still my heart and thoughts. I am going to allow myself to be in Your presence and rest in You, knowing You are gracious and compassionate. Knowing You will work out Your plans for my life. Help me center my heart and my thoughts and my very life on You. Help me live vitally connected to You and quiet on the inside so I can always hear You and walk in the power of Your amazing presence and Your amazing peace. In the mighty name of Jesus, amen.

HEART NOTES

_____

_____

_____

_____

_____

92

Holy Expectancy

Wait and hope for and expect the Lord;
be brave and of good courage
and let your heart be stout and enduring.
Yes, wait for and hope for and expect the Lord.

PSALM 27:14 AMPC

Waiting isn't anyone's favorite thing. We await a baby's birth and a response about a recent job interview. We wait for updates concerning a loved one's surgery, for vacation days to arrive, and for news from an overseas soldier. Waiting challenges our patience, is unpleasant, and places our hearts in suspense, often taking much longer than we hope or like, which can stir anxiety in our souls.

And yet, there exists a holy waiting, one that persists with an uplifted heart because its focus is on a mighty, sovereign, and powerful God. We can wait with a holy expectancy, knowing that God is good and faithful and always at work despite how things may appear. Understanding this enables us to be brave even when we experience uncomfortable or unexpected delays. Because we anticipate God's move, our hearts can be stout and enduring and filled with peace even while we wait. We can wait with the assurance that He is good and faithful and working all things for our good because we love Him (Romans 8:28). As we allow our hearts to be brave in the wait, He gives us grace to endure and keeps us in His peace.

Lord, I choose to be a believer who waits with holy expectancy and who expects You to intervene in the matters that deeply concern me. Will You please give me grace to wait with a good attitude and a hopeful, uplifted heart? As I wait, may my heart's focus be on You, Lord. You are awesome and mighty, and nothing is impossible for You. Fill my heart with faith and help me be brave while I wait, expecting You to move as only You can. Give me grace to endure. May my heart be stout and enduring and filled with Your peace. In the awesome name of Jesus, amen.

HEART NOTES

_____

_____

_____

_____

_____

_____

93

Your Weakness, Christ's Power

Each time he said, "My grace is all you need. My
power works best in weakness." So now I am
glad to boast about my weaknesses, so that
the power of Christ can work through me.

2 CORINTHIANS 12:9

t is a natural human tendency to think we must have it all
together or else we simply cannot do what God seems to be
requiring of us. Like hosting a book study on marriage when
ours is not perfect. Like inviting a friend to church when our
faith still feels so small. Or like fighting the Midianites when
you're the least in your family (see Judges 6:15). Gideon's clan
was the weakest of Israel's tribes, and he was the least in his entire
family. And yet God chose Gideon to fight the cruel Midianites, assuring him, "I will be with you" (verse 16). And He was.

We wrestle with our weaknesses, wondering how we can
accomplish what is at hand, only to discover that we are precisely where God wants us. Inexplicably, His power works best
in our weakness. He uses us despite our inabilities. What a
relief! We don't have to be perfect. We don't have to be strong,
and we don't have to have it all together. God assures us that all

we need is His grace, which He lavishly provides. In whatever state we currently find ourselves, it is well. Christ's power can work through us.

Lord, when I recognize my own inabilities and ineffectiveness, please help me not to be discouraged or to panic. Help me rely continually on Your abundant grace, knowing that it is truly all I need. Lord, may Your power, love, and goodness be showcased in me—not because I am able or gifted or having a good, anxiety-free day, but so Your awesome power can be displayed. I do not understand it, but oh, Lord, thank You. Thank You for using me despite my inabilities and for working in my weakness. In Jesus's name, amen.

HEART NOTES

_____

_____

_____

_____

_____

94

Every Detail

Do not be afraid or discouraged, for the LORD
will personally go ahead of you. He will be with
you; he will neither fail you nor abandon you.

DEUTERONOMY 31:8

How immensely encouraging and comforting it is to know that God Himself personally goes before us. Absolutely nothing takes Him by surprise. When we're uncertain or confused, He is consistently steady and near. When our closest friend moves out of state, when our job description changes dramatically, and on days when tears sting our eyes more than once, we don't have to allow anxiety to get the best of us.

When uneasiness clatters against our hearts, how reassuring it is to know that the Lord is with us and for us, clearing the way ahead. He knows every turn and all the details of our path, and in His kindness and goodness He orchestrates the specifics that deeply concern our hearts. Through each disappointment or setback, He never fails us or abandons us.

Nothing in life remains constant, and course changes inevitably happen. Yet, "Jesus Christ is the same yesterday, today, and forever" (Hebrews 13:8). He is the solid Rock our hearts lean on when the unexpected occurs. We never have to fret or yield to apprehension, because whatever each day holds, He is with us—His beautiful presence leading, calming, and reassuring us every step of the way.

Lord, I'm grateful that You see the big picture in my life, and yet You still oversee even the smallest of details. When unexpected changes happen, help me remember that You go before me in all I do, orchestrating all that concerns my heart, planning my way today and every day. Because You oversee everything, never failing me or abandoning me, I can choose to resist apprehension and rest in your faithfulness. I love that Your awesome, mighty presence leads me, reassures me, and calms me. You are the solid Rock stabilizing my heart, and I am grateful. In Jesus's precious name, amen.

HEART NOTES

_____

_____

_____

_____

_____

95

Releasing Your Worries

Give all your worries and cares to
God, for he cares about you.

1 PETER 5:7

Why do we persist in tightly holding on to everything that upsets us, makes us edgy, or stirs up anxious feelings in our hearts? Could it be that relinquishing is so tough for us because we struggle to completely trust God? Our heavenly Father loves us, affectionately caring for us and watching over us, and He invites us to toss every worry—throwing each one hard and strong—straight into His hands. Just like hurling a rock from the lakeshore far out into the deep, where we are not in danger of retrieving it.

When releasing our worries to God feels arduous, remembering His character will absolutely help us. The Lord is gracious and compassionate. He is kind and holy and all-powerful. And in His great love for us He desires that we live life without an 80-pound rucksack of worries on our back. We can entrust everything to Him and experience freedom from all that troubles us. Instead of holding on to our worries, let's cling tightly to God's goodness, love, hope, joy, and peace.

Lord, please teach me not to hold on to all that frustrates me, makes me uneasy, or stirs up anxiety in my heart. Right now I choose to lift each of my concerns to You, entrusting them into Your sovereign care once and for all. When I struggle to release my cares to You, please give me grace to trust You. Help me not take back my worries but entrust each one to You, knowing You are good and kind and all-powerful. Prompt me by Your Spirit the moment I am tempted to retrieve any worry or concern. Thank You for carrying all I cannot. Thank You for loving me, caring for me, and watching over me. In Jesus's name, amen.

HEART NOTES

_____

_____

_____

_____

_____

96

Freed

I prayed to the LORD, and he answered me.
He freed me from all my fears.

PSALM 34:4

Fears can be so sneaky, subtle, and hidden. For instance, insecurity is a type of fear that might cause us to avoid a conversation with strangers at a neighborhood park or a friend's party. An underlying fear of being wrong could stop us from sharing what we know or speaking our minds. And fear is definitely the primary motivating factor behind our control issues.

If we would recognize it sooner, we could resist it. This is exactly why we pray, inviting the Lord into our doubts and fears, asking Him for wisdom and understanding. God knows the fears we battle—and when we pray, He answers us. He intervenes, filling our hearts with His light and truth, displacing the darkness that fear tries to bring. Prayer brings divine perspective and fills our hearts with courage.

Through prayer the Lord gives us insight and clarity so we can recognize fear's tactics and resist them, turning to Jesus instead. He helps us live bravely. He is the foundation we can count on, and even when dread makes us quake, He keeps us stable. The Lord not only hears us, but He also leads us from fear toward freedom. He covers us with His presence and frees us from all our fears.

> *Lord, You know the fears I battle. You even know the subtle fears that, though I hardly recognize them because they are so deep and hidden, still manage to steer and shape me. But Lord, I long for freedom from every fear. Please give me wisdom and discernment in this area. Thank You that as I turn to You, my stable foundation, You give me insight and clarity so I can always resist fear's tactics. Thank You for displacing every fear in my heart, filling me with Your light and truth. I'm grateful that You are greater than every fear. You not only hear me, but You lead me into freedom. You free me from every fear. In Your name I pray, amen.*

HEART NOTES

_____

_____

_____

_____

97

Your Safe Place

Trust in, lean on, rely on, and have confidence in Him at
all times, you people; pour out your hearts before Him.
God is a refuge for us (a fortress and a high tower).

PSALM 62:8 AMPC

God wants us to rely on Him at all times—every time we
receive bad news, every time circumstances look uncertain, and every time we're *this close* to a meltdown. This is how
trusting Him becomes a holy instinct, our automatic response
to adversity and hardships. We must rely on Him more than
our spouse or our closest friend. We must habitually turn to
Him first.

The Lord invites us to pour out our hearts to Him, and we
must take advantage of that invitation. One of the ways we do
this is through honest prayer. Raw prayer. Tear-filled prayer that
holds nothing back. David, the author of this psalm (and many
others), prayed this way. He understood that our good heavenly
Father is a safe place—the fortress where we can go to vent all
that has piled up deep inside us.

The Lord understands us and wants us to feel confident in
His love for us. Those anxious feelings that threaten to overwhelm us? They're no match for the Lord. He is our awesome

high tower, and our hearts are secure, protected, and filled with His peace when we run to Him.

> *Lord, please teach me to be consistent in running to You when I need to vent. May trusting and relying on You become a holy instinct for me. Help me be honest and habitually pour out my heart to You because You are my safe place. You understand me, and I can feel confident in Your love for me. Help me trust You, lean on You, and rely on You, since You are my fortress, faithful and utterly trustworthy. Thank You for loving me, soothing my heart, and being the secure place of refuge my heart so desperately needs. In Jesus's name, amen.*

HEART NOTES

_____

_____

_____

_____

_____

98

Pursued by Goodness and Love

Surely your goodness and unfailing love will
pursue me all the days of my life, and I will
live in the house of the LORD forever.

PSALM 23:6

How reassuring to know that God's goodness and unfailing love are not static. They are active and moving because He is active and moving. God *is* love (1 John 4:8); therefore, this awesome God who *is* love cannot help but pursue us. He loves us, sings over us, and longs for us. He pursues us on our best days and our worst. He pursues us when we think of Him and when we do not. Every day of our lives He pursues us, drawing us to Him, reaching out to our anxious hearts so we can experience His unfailing love.

On days when we're inundated with problems or decisions that stoke uneasiness, God is with us. His love is a strong, calming force in our sometimes-frantic lives. Zephaniah 3:17 says, "The LORD your God is living among you. He is a mighty savior. He will take delight in you with gladness. With his love, he will calm all your fears. He will rejoice over you with joyful songs." God is always with us. He *delights* in us! His unfailing love calms all that shakes within us, filling our hearts with His priceless peace.

Lord, I'm amazed that in Your goodness and love You actively and consistently pursue me. Every day of my life You pursue me! Will You please give me a receptive and tender heart toward You? One that is open and responsive to Your pursuit of me and willing and eager to rest in You? Thank You for loving me and delighting in me. Thank You for singing over me. Thank You for longing for me. Thank You for calming all my fears and teaching my heart to rest in Your unfailing love. In Jesus's name, amen.

HEART NOTES

_____

_____

_____

_____

_____

99

Seeing with Faith

Now faith is confidence in what we hope for
and assurance about what we do not see.

HEBREWS 11:1 NIV

Living a faith-filled life requires us to see through the eyes of
faith. This doesn't mean that we live in denial of the facts,
but rather that we absolutely trust God is at work and believe
what He says, sometimes in spite of what's before our eyes.

So even as we deal with the reality of anxiety in our lives and
all its ripple effects, we can choose to stand and believe that God
is a God who hears our prayers, heals our hearts, and brings us
into freedom in Christ. On really bad days we can retain our
hope instead of plunging into despair. Though our hearts struggle, we can hold on to our confidence that God is faithful and
dependable.

As 2 Corinthians 5:7 (NIV) says, "We live by faith, not by
sight." We do this by choosing to believe that God is greater
than all our inner turmoil and uneasiness. That He is stronger
than the fears raging inside us. As we live by faith we are choosing to live in His peace, because we entrust absolutely everything to Him. When current conditions demand our attention,
may the eyes of our hearts nonetheless see with faith.

Lord, I am determined to be a person of faith—not because of what I see, but in spite of it; not because I deny the facts, but because I absolutely trust that You are working in me, and I believe what You say. You say I am healed. You say I am whole. You are at work in my heart, freeing me from every fear, neutralizing anxiety's effects. Because You are faithful, I can entrust everything to You. You are greater and stronger than all my inner turmoil and the fears that sometimes rage inside me. Thank You for helping me live by faith and for filling me with Your unfathomable peace. In Jesus's name, amen.

HEART NOTES

_____

_____

_____

_____

_____

100

We Can Laugh

She is clothed with strength and dignity,
and she laughs without fear of the future.

PROVERBS 31:25

We are people of faith who know the living God. We know He is our good heavenly Father and we belong to Him. We are people who believe in, trust in, and rely on the finished work of the cross. We believe in and cling to Jesus Christ, God's only Son. We are people who yield to the Holy Spirit, who leads us into all truth (John 16:13). We are people "clothed with strength and dignity." Because God is moving in our lives and freeing our hearts, we can laugh without fear.

Even though our situations are not perfect, we can have joy. We can live good, productive, beautiful lives. Instead of holding back, we can take that next step with great courage. Instead of quitting or running the other way, we can persevere and do the hard thing. Instead of allowing anxiety to control us, we can pray, draw near to God, trust Him, and experience every ounce of peace Jesus died to give us. Whatever life throws our way, may His holy laughter fill our hearts and homes. And may we live boldly because we do not fear the future.

*Lord, when I am tempted to feel weak and insignificant,
I will remember what You say about me: I am loved, I am
redeemed, and I am Your precious child. I know You—
the living God. I rely on Jesus's finished work at the cross.
I yield to Your Spirit, who leads me into all truth. I am
clothed with strength and dignity. Thank You for moving
in my life as only You can. Thank You for freeing my
heart from every ounce of anxiety. Thank You for enabling
me to laugh without fear and to do all You lead me to
do because I have no fear of the future. I have You. And
I have Your amazing peace. In Jesus's name, amen.*

HEART NOTES

_____

_____

_____

_____

_____

Personal Prayer Page

_____

_____

_____

_____

_____

_____

_____

_____

_____

_____

_____

_____

_____

_____

_____

_____

_____

Personal Prayer Page

_____

_____

_____

_____

_____

_____

_____

_____

_____

_____

_____

_____

_____

_____

_____

_____

Personal Prayer Page

_____

_____

_____

_____

_____

_____

_____

_____

_____

_____

_____

_____

_____

_____

_____

Personal Prayer Page

_____

_____

_____

_____

_____

_____

_____

_____

_____

_____

_____

_____

_____

_____

_____

_____

_____

_____

Personal Prayer Page

_____

_____

_____

_____

_____

_____

_____

_____

_____

_____

_____

_____

_____

_____

_____

_____

_____

_____

Personal Prayer Page

_____

_____

_____

_____

_____

_____

_____

_____

_____

_____

_____

_____

_____

_____

_____

_____

_____

Personal Prayer Page

_____

_____

_____

_____

_____

_____

_____

_____

_____

_____

_____

_____

_____

_____

_____

_____

Personal Prayer Page

_____
_____
_____
_____
_____
_____
_____
_____
_____
_____
_____
_____
_____
_____
_____
_____
_____